Evangelizing the New Age

*The Power of the Gospel Invades
the New Age Movement*

Paul McGuire

VB
VINE
BOOKS

Servant Publications
Ann Arbor, Michigan

Vine Books is an imprint of Servant Publications especially
designed to serve Evangelical Christians.

Published by Servant Publications
P.O. Box 8617
Ann Arbor, Michigan 48107

Cover design by Michael Andaloro & Jamie Adams
Cover Illustration by Jamie Adams

89 90 91 92 93 10 9 8 7 6 5 4 3 2 1

Printed in the United States of America
ISBN 0-89283-633-4

Library of Congress Cataloging-in-Publication Data

McGuire, Paul, 1953-
    Evangelizing the New Age : the power of the gospel
invades the New Age movement / by Paul McGuire.
        p. cm.
    Bibliography : p.
    ISBN 0-89283-633-4
    1. New Age movement—Controversial
literature.   2. Evangelistic work—United States.   I. Title.
BP605.N48M38   1989
299′.93—dc20   89-33977
                                                      CIP

Contents

Acknowledgements

To Beth Feia whose vision and persistence guided this book and to Ann Spangler, Mary Case, and the people at Servant Publications.

To Kay Mangio and the Full Gospel Business Men's Fellowship International, my pastor Reverend Jack Hayford, Reverend Scott Bauer, Reverend Jim Tolle, Keith Dawson, and all my brothers and sisters at The Church On The Way.

To Mom, Dad, Frances, Laura, Caitlin, John, Jack, Camie, Grandmere, Denny, Kathy, Michael, and Justin.

Foreword

HOW ELECTRIC IS OUR CHRISTIANITY?

The course of all human history was changed nearly 2,000 years ago, when a Man died on a Cross. But with all its triumph, Calvary is timeless, *its powerful current inevitably touching every human life and death.* Yet, too many still fail to feel its pulsating power.

Jesus Christ not only *represents* life at its richest, he *is* life in all its vitality and abundance. Yet, more and more spiritually hungry Americans are turning, not to Christianity for healing and fulfillment, but to Eastern mysticism—the New Age philosophy, which has snaked its way into the boardrooms of corporate America and even into high levels of our nation's government.

Paul McGuire says that today's church has failed to exemplify the vibrant life and unconditional love of Jesus Christ. In the following pages, he calls the church of Jesus Christ to relinquish the relics of its past, remove its preoccupying focus from thrilling prophecies about the future, and minister to a spiritually hungry world *today.* He reminds us as members of the church to do so in a way that communicates the vitality and timeliness, the power, life, and love of the Lord himself.

And here we see the role of the Holy Spirit and his gifts in accomplishing the church's divine directive to reach the lost. Jesus Christ—God's vital spirituality— is made real to us by the present ministry of the Holy Spirit. Only supernatural living, impassioned by the Spirit's presence, tempered by Christ's love, and founded on the eternal, unchanging Word of God, can overpower the insidious, seductive ways of the New Age. Paul McGuire repeatedly turns to the Scriptures to highlight clear instructions about how to fight spiritual battles, how to preach the Gospel, and how to relate to New Age thinking.

Evangelizing the New Age is not a call to paranoia but to compassion and loving communication. It's a call to believers to become disciples, to step out of their pews and into the trenches. I am grateful to be called Paul's pastor. He and his wife, Kristina, are consistent, dedicated believers who live what they talk, and talk what they live. I'm glad for this book. Any believer who wants to answer Christ's call to reclaim his city and nation for Jesus Christ will be stimulated and taught by these pages. God help us to be instruments of vibrant, sterling electricity in a dark hour when pure light—not black—is needed.

Jack W. Hayford, Senior Pastor
The Church On The Way
Van Nuys, California

ONE

The Search

THE SUN WAS SETTING on the island paradise of Maui. I was vacationing aboard a forty-eight-foot sailing yacht called "Genesis." As its captain piloted this vessel through the waters, I held my wife's hand and looked up at the heavens with their swirling galaxy of stars and the crescent moon which loomed over the island sky. I felt as if I were Adam at the very beginning of time, and my thoughts turned naturally to God as the stars shimmered with light. For the believer in Jesus Christ there are no accidents, and it was no coincidence that I was on a yacht in paradise whose name, "Genesis," spoke of the beginning of time and God's creation of the world.

Thoughts raced through my mind concerning the great spiritual search that was going on all over the world and the emergence of what the media has termed the New Age Movement. As I gazed upon the celestial brilliance of the crystal clear evening sky of Maui, I meditated on the fact that the living God so designed creation that it speaks of him and that all men and women staring up at the night sky must sooner or later begin to contemplate the reasons for their existence and ask the questions: Who am I? What is my purpose in life? Who is God?

The island of Maui was exploding like the volcano which had created it, only this time with spiritual activity. Leaders of the New Age Movement had come to the island to give seminars on channeling and crystals. New Age pilgrims had built little rock monuments on the cliffs facing the water in the hope of contacting visitors from outer space. A lady named Sapphire Moon was available for private spiritual consultation, and famous doctors like Dr. Stanley Krippner had come to the island to discuss the power in creating your personal mythology.

It seemed as if Maui was a microcosm of the United States and the Western world, for it had attracted what has been termed the "baby boom" generation, those who have enjoyed more material affluence and education than any other generation in the history of mankind, and who are yet in search of spiritual answers. Even the crew of the boat represented the spiritual hunger of our times: Captain Sean had sailed the world and been exposed to the religions of the Orient, and Neal, now in his mid-twenties, had been reared in Tennessee on The Farm commune, led by the American guru Stephen Gaskin. While most American kids were watching television, Neal was chanting *OM* with hundreds of members of The Farm. He was a product of the spiritual search of the earlier hippie movement of the 1960s. Neal's mother had recently found Jesus Christ and had become part of Wallace and Marilyn Hickey's church in Colorado. Having surrendered his life to Jesus Christ only two-and-a-half years earlier, Neal himself had many questions concerning his faith in Jesus Christ as we sailed aboard the "Genesis."

The people I talked to on my trip to Maui left me reflecting on the spiritual confusion that enslaves so many searching people and the incredible spiritual awakening I experienced when my search ended in the arms of a loving God. I grew up in New York City in a well-educated family that embraced the dual philosophies of secular humanism and scientific materialism. For me, like many of the people in the current New Age Movement, Christianity had not even been a viable option. I was taught that Christians were anti-sex, anti-joy, and anti-life, and that Christianity was a primitive religion which should be transcended by all thinking and intelligent people. When my family joined together for dinner, instead of praying we would begin discussing the teachings of Friedrich Nietzsche, whose writings inspired the "God is Dead" movement.

However, at a young age I recognized that there had to be more to life than simply a material existence, and so after studying the lives of many great scientists I began to investigate the world of pyschic research, Eastern mysticism, and the books of Aldous Huxley and Edgar Cayce, all of which encourage people to travel through the "doors of perception." In a further effort to find the answers to life's most important questions, I entered psychotherapy. These were my small and seemingly harmless introductions to what is now called the New Age Movement, and I spent over a decade involved in Hinduism, Buddhism, astral projection, mental telepathy, meditation, yoga, psychedelic drugs, Zen enlightenment, cosmic consciousness, and "inner space" travel. Eventually, after attending a Christian retreat, I accepted Jesus Christ while hitchhiking on the back roads of Columbia, Missouri. At that time a "cosmic seed" was planted in my life which changed me forever, and I recognized that there was a radical difference between the teachings of Jesus Christ and all the New Age activities I was involved in.

TROUBLE ON SPACESHIP EARTH

You and I live on a spinning sphere called Earth, which orbits the sun in a place called the universe. In a sense, each of us is a cosmic traveler who temporarily inhabits what inventor and scientist Buckminister Fuller called Spaceship Earth. Even to the casual observer it is clear that there is a crisis on the spaceship and that all of us are in mortal danger. The threats of nuclear holocaust, AIDS, pollution, famine, and economic collapse loom over us, dimming our hope of creating a paradise on our home planet.

In the midst of this crisis, we desperately search for answers, and we find that modern science, Western systems of logic and reason, and massive technology are unable to save us. In the calm before the storm of the apocalypse, the human race is mobilizing all of its energies and forces in a brave attempt to transcend the imprisoning limitations of linear thought patterns and to evolve into the infinite and higher consciousness of what many have called the great New Age.

Within this powerful cultural milieu we find that millions of people between the ages of fifteen and forty-five years have turned their backs on the claims of Jesus Christ and have embraced ancient Babylonian, Hindu, and Buddhist philosophies repackaged to communicate to the modern world by using high-tech and scientific terms. Millions of people in our world have been severely alienated by Christianity and do not consider it a viable option. It is not that people are not spiritually hungry. The explosive growth of the New Age Movement reveals that an entire generation is desperate for answers, so desperate that they will flock to Eastern gurus, channelers, and crystals for answers before they will darken the door of a Christian church.

TROUBLE IN THE CHRISTIAN WORLD

When this generation pressed its face to the windows of the Christian church and found unbelief, a denial of the supernatural reality of the living God of the universe, dead orthodoxy, ritualism, and financial manipulation, rather than the vibrant life of the living Christ, it rejected Christianity. These people chose not to visit a museum called Christianity, and instead opted in favor of the immediate spiritual reality of the New Age.

In recent years there have been great revivals through both the evangelical and the charismatic movements, and millions around the world have turned to Jesus Christ. But I believe that this is only a small part of what God wants to do. I believe that we are on the verge of a revival in which millions of people will be swept into the kingdom of God. But I do not believe that this will just "happen." This revival will only come as God's people remove from their midst the hindrances to this revival and join with the Holy Spirit to become living agents of this revival upon our planet. In other words, we must cooperate with Jesus in allowing the power of the Holy Spirit to flow upon this world through our individual lives.

SPEAKING IN THE LANGUAGE OF THE PEOPLE

I also believe Jesus wants us to stop talking about him as if he were still wandering around Galilee in ancient Israel. Jesus is not roaming Israel wearing a long garment and sandals. He is sitting on his throne at the right hand of the Father. He is Lord of the past, present, and future, and although there is much we can learn from studying his earthly ministry, it is time for the church of Jesus Christ to appropriate the lessons of his past earthly ministry for the *present* ministry that God has for each of us on earth right now. We are to serve our present Lord as well as the past and future Christ.

Our Lord is often represented as a remnant of an ancient and long-dead Middle Eastern society, when in truth he is more current and viable than anything our computers, gene splicing, high-definition television, fiber optics, and nuclear energy could imagine or produce. We must learn to speak to our culture in the language of our day, not in the language of yesterday. Part of the reason why the Eastern mystical philosophies of the New Age have gained such widespread acceptance is that their proponents have learned to dust off these ancient Hindu and Buddhist mythologies and dress them up in contemporary psychological terms.

In light of the significant growth of Eastern religions and New Age practices, such as yoga, meditation, astrology, and channeling, it is obvious that people are spiritually hungry but that they are not interested in church. I believe that this problem exists because a large number of churches are no longer moving in the power of the Holy Spirit and have therefore managed to make themselves irrelevant. Ironically, New Age religions have learned how to use supernatural power to meet the needs of people at the same time that many churches have rejected a supernatural reality in favor of materialism. If the church of Jesus Christ is to obey his command to "Go into all the world and preach the gospel to all creation" (Mk 16:15), then we must earnestly seek answers to this question: How can we effectively reach this post-Christian culture and those involved in Eastern mysticism and the New Age?

THE NEW AGE RAMPAGE

Marilyn Ferguson has authored what many people consider the handbook for the New Age and Higher Consciousness Movement—*The Aquarian Conspiracy.* Ferguson also is publisher of the "Brain/Mind Bulletin," which has been referred to as the most widely read newsletter in the areas of humanistic medicine, memory, learning, creativity, brain research, biofeedback, pain, and the physics of consciousness. She is an intellectual powerhouse of New Age thinking who has managed to link Eastern mysticism with cutting-edge scientific research.

Ferguson's previous book, *The Brain Revolution,* has helped to establish what she terms "The Aquarian Conspiracy," a global network of advanced thinkers including Nobel laureate scientists, philosophers, statesmen, celebrities, and steadily growing numbers from every segment of society. Ferguson conceived of the term "Aquarian Conspiracy" from Greek novelist Nikos Kazantzakis who authored both *Zorba the Greek* and the controversial *The Last Temptation of Christ.* In 1927, Kazantzakis envisioned a union of individuals, "those who might create for earth a brain and heart, might give a human meaning to the superhuman struggle," comrades he might signal "with a password like conspirators." What we have called God is the evolutionary drive of the consciousness in the universe, he believed. "The new earth only exists in the heart of man."[1]

In her book Ferguson outlines:

... how an underground network is working to create a different kind of society based on a vastly enlarged concept of human potential. ... how the technologies for expanding personal consciousness, once the secret of an elite, are now generating massive change in every cultural institution—medicine, politics, business, education, religion, and the family.[2]

Ferguson says,

We are not so much haunted by events as by our beliefs about them, the crippling self-image we take with us. We can transform the present and the future by reawakening the powerful past, with its recurrent message of defeat. We can face the crossroads again. We can re-choose. In a similar spirit, we can respond differently to the tragedies of modern history. Our past is not our potential. In any hour, with all the stubborn teachers and healers of history who called us to be our best selves, we can liberate the future. One by one we can re-choose—to awaken. To leave the prison of our conditioning, to love, to turn homeward. To conspire with and for each other.[3]

If we listen carefully, we can hear in Marilyn Ferguson's words the pounding optimism of the New Age and Higher Consciousness Movement. As biblical Christians it is important that we, too, affirm that which is beautiful and noble within the human race. Then we must learn how to communicate intelligently, compassionately, and truthfully to our fellowmen about the biblical worldview, and with the skill of a surgeon performing open heart surgery we must present the truth of the gospel of Jesus Christ to our fellow men. We need to let others know that true release of human potential resides in only one person—the Savior Jesus Christ.

Neither the anti-intellectual preaching which is present in much of contemporary Christianity nor the powerless intellectual and liberal theological expositions have done much to reach the Marilyn Fergusons of our time. In all honesty, we must admit that people like Ferguson are far better evangelists for their religion than many so-called Christian evangelists. The preachers who consider magazines like *Scientific American* to be pornography and who define Christianity by negating the world are no match for the likes of Ferguson, who is respected by scientists and world leaders alike. It is not that "The Aquarian Conspiracy" is true and that Christianity is a primitive level of consciousness that should be transcended. It is that so much of American Christianity has become a comfortable social experience that lacks any real challenge to change lives for the better. This is not the gospel of the kingdom that Jesus taught.

THE BATTLE FOR CORPORATE AMERICA

The New Age Movement and the philosophies of secular humanism have infiltrated corporate America. In a quest for greater profits and productivity, CEOs and high-powered executives have turned to the New Age and to humanistic pyschologists.

In the preface to *Behavioral Supervision: Practical Ways to Change Behavior and Increase Productivity*, author Les Donaldson explains:

> The key concepts of B.F. Skinner, blended with the theories of Freud, Lefton, Maslow, Minnick, McClelland, Nirenberg, and Carl Rogers, form the framework for a practical approach to changing unsatisfactory on-the-job behavior. You can use these key techniques to become a more effective supervisor by gaining cooperation, overcoming performance slumps, correcting uncooperative subordinate behavior patterns, and dealing with argumentative or sarcastic people.[4]

The fact that the philosophical foundation for these corporate management techniques comes from humanistic philosophies does not mean that these ideas do not work or that they are all bad ideas. Many of the management techniques in this book are effective. That's not the point. In all these new forms of management the primary problem is lack of any clear Judeo-Christian or biblical teaching. As Christians, we have not communicated biblical truths as something relevant to American business. Humanistic psychology and New Age techniques have rushed in to fill the philosophical gap left by Christianity when it deserted business and the other power centers of our society. The result is New Age distortions at the highest levels.

In their mad dash for greater profits many American corporations have embraced the New Age and the occult. According to a recent *Omni* magazine article entitled "The Omni WholeMind Newsletter: A User's Manual to the Brain, Mind, and Spirit": "Psychics and stockbrokers would seem to be strange bedfellows. But their alliance is becoming a fact of business." The article goes on to say that there is an increasing relationship between big business, astrologers, and psychics. "Financial astrologer Arch Crawford, formerly a Merrill Lynch analyst, charges $250 for ten annual issues of his newsletter. For $2,500 a year you can call him anytime; otherwise it's $100 a call. That sounds pretty stiff until you look at his record. *Timer Digest*, which rates the trader newsletters, put him on the cover of its April/May issue, calling him the second most accurate forecaster of 1986."[5]

WERNER ERHARD AND TRANSFORMATIONAL TECHNOLOGIES

Werner Erhard, the founder of est, The Forum, and a New Age management consulting firm called Transformational Technologies, has been called by Mark MacNamara of *Los*

Angeles Magazine "the first American guru, a salesman turned spiritualist, a clever craftsman who understood how to combine pop philosophies, Eastern religions and the Puritan work ethic into an effective way to motivate people."[6]

Werner Erhard grew up as Jack Rosenberg, changed his name first to Jack Frost while he was a car salesman in Pennsylvania, and then to Werner Erhard after a spiritual transformation. Werner Erhard, or Jack Rosenberg, was born to an Episcopalian mother and a fundamentalist Christian father. After rejecting the religion of his father, Werner Erhard studied Zen, Dale Carnegie, Buddhism, and numerous other disciplines before starting est (Erhard Seminars Training). The purpose of est, which lasted from 1971 to 1984, was "to get people to move, see themselves in a new way, disregard all the old tapes, and start life over again."[7]

As a sophisticated marketeer Erhard enrolled over 600,000 people worldwide in his est or Forum training programs. In addition, he broadcast a Satellite Seminar Series in over twenty-six major cities. Graduates of est and the Forum have been responsible for introducing Erhard's philosophy to an even wider audience via the advertising industry by creating slogans like "Master the Possibilities" for Master-Card and "Commitment, Integrity and Vision" for Shearson-Lehman. Werner has developed several spin-off companies, such as a management consulting business started in 1984 called Transformational Technologies; Werner Erhard and Associates, which sponsors The Forum; The Holiday Project, which has organized 20,000 volunteers in 100 cities who visit prisons, nursing homes, hospitals, psychiatric facilities, and shelters for battered women and children; The Werner Erhard Foundation, an international crisis relief group which raised over $65,000 for earthquake victims in Mexico City; The Hunger Project, a grass-roots organization to end world hunger; The Breakthrough Foundation to help juvenile delinquents; and The Mastery Foundation that trains religious ministers and offers the course "Making a Difference: A Course for Those Who Minister and the Education Network."[8]

Erhard's organizations pull in about $35 million per year, and his new effort, Transformational Technologies, is now teaching New Age-oriented techniques to 100 of the Fortune 500 companies according to New Age expert Tal Brooke, author of *Riders of the Cosmic Circuit.* Carl Raschke, professor of Religion at the University of Denver, said, "Werner has developed one of the most successful marketing tools of New Age consciousness-raising ever developed." Raschke concluded,

Is it good or bad? If you believe that the preservation of traditional American social values and religious ideals and commitment is a good thing, then what Erhard has done is utterly disastrous because the whole purpose of est was to disengage you from hang-ups, from loyalties to groups, individuals, and institutions, and make you thoroughly responsible to yourself. On the other hand, if you believe America suffers from an encrusted and obsolete set of moral-authoritarian values and the whole nature of traditional religious expression, patriotism, philanthropy, and personal allegiance is keeping American society from moving into a New Age millennium, then Erhard is doing a good thing.[9]

Erhard's Transformational Technologies and a multitude of other New Age-oriented companies are penetrating the bastions of capitalism with Eastern mysticism packaged as "management training." The bottom line is that it doesn't do much good to sit on the outside and criticize what people like Werner Erhard are doing. Christians who criticize how the New Age Movement is infiltrating corporate America miss the whole point. People like Erhard and other New Age teachers are successful because they are providing answers and speaking in the language of the day. The real issue isn't Werner Erhard and how he is selling New Age techniques to major corporations. The real issue is, why aren't Christians addressing the needs of corporate America?

Christians who adopt a retreatist position allow the New Age to rush in and fill the spiritual vacuum. When Christianity no longer preaches the same gospel of the kingdom that Jesus Christ preached, counterfeit philosophies take its place. The only answer to this situation is to preach the same gospel Jesus did! Sitting around and pointing the finger just won't work. Only the light will dispel the darkness.

THE PENTAGON MEDITATION CLUB

It is Friday 11:30 A.M. and from the very inner sanctums of the nation's Pentagon come the chants of *OM*. A speaker says:

We image our world leaders coming together—all influential leaders, spiritual leaders, religious leaders at all levels, joining together, resolving issues, resolving conflicts, learning to communicate with one another. We're conscious of the divine light radiating from within our being, the light of life shining out into the courtyard, into this building, filling it with the light of life, touching everyone we meet, everyone who isn't here. . . . We expand the vision to include the entire nation, then expand it to include every part of the world, particularly military installations scattered around the world.[10]

Then the speaker urges the participants to "call to your awareness your holy word, your name for God, which can be anything that represents the divinity to you," such as Jesus, Christ, Buddha, Adonai, YHWH, Jehovah, Allah, Ram, Brahman, Sat-Naam, Radha-Krishna, Bahaullah, Aum (or *OM*), or Great Spirit. The Pentagon Meditation Club was founded by scientist Ed Winchester; he applied his theories of creative intelligence to the Pentagon management systems and evolved the practice from Transcendental Meditation. The purpose of the Pentagon Meditation Club is to launch a Spiritual Defensive Initiative (SDI) or "peace shield of energy and light all over the planet."[11]

Winchester advocates that a combination of meditation and creative visualization techniques be exercised by the meditators. During a Reagan-Gorbachev summit, Ed Winchester led a contingent of Soviets in a twenty-minute meditation and creative visualization exercise for world peace. The Club attracted world media attention when it escorted the twelve Soviets into the Pentagon's executive dining room for their annual Prayer Breakfast. Over 400 military personnel, members of the Soviet Central Peace Committee, and clergy were in attendance.

Ed Winchester has introduced his theories of creative intelligence to the Lorton Correctional Facility, a prison in Washington, D.C. He got the Pentagon to back a prison project called "Experiment in Organizational Transformation" which dealt with overcrowding, budget deficits, and unrest in prisons. Over the course of the program more than 1200 inmates and officers were trained in meditation, and once violent criminals began planting flower gardens in the facility.

Due to his success, Winchester has the support of people like Barbara Carpenter, a psychotherapist and organizer of Washington, D.C.'s Network of Light. Barbara Carpenter shares Winchester's vision of a peace shield for planet earth and is helping him organize an International Network of Light; they already have people meditating in places like Japan, Taiwan, Korea, Scotland, England, France, and China. Guru Sri Chinmoy, who is responsible for the meditation activities at the United Nations, is scheduled to visit the Club in the Pentagon.

Eastern mystical thinking has advanced into the upper echelons of the U.S. government. Where are the Christians?

MODERN SHAMANISM

People from every walk of life are tapping into this wave of spiritualism in an effort to address human problems. Take the growth of Shamanism for example. Shamanism is the ancient tradition of using altered states of consciousness to bring about a change in reality or a spiritual healing. A shaman may use mental powers through processes like guided imagery, visualization, and trance states to heal people physically and mentally. Shamanism is many centuries old and is prevalent in the cultures of Japan, Africa, Asia, and Hawaii.

In Okinawa, the practice of shamanism is still very strong. Recent studies have indicated that two out of every three Okinawans have consulted a shaman. Tokutaro Sakurai, president of Tokyo's Komazawa University and an authority on Okinawan religion, said, "Shamanism is a universal phenomenon surfacing in various isolated strains in most cultures around the world, including the United States, where it is seen in American Indian beliefs and in the spirit possession of some Christian sects."[12] Sakurai added that he is fascinated by actress Shirley MacLaine's "shamanistic tendencies" in her writing.

Contemporary America is now experiencing a burgeoning shamanistic movement through the teachings of people like Lynn Andrews, Shirley MacLaine, and Carlos Castaneda. Modern shamans often receive their training from the ancient Hawaiian practice of Huna, a philosophy of the powers of the mind and how they interreact with the forces of nature. According to Serge King, a Western-trained psychologist and writer who trained as a shaman healer in Hawaii and Africa, there are seven basic elements to Huna. It is interesting to note that these seven principles of Huna or Hawaiian shamanism are vital ingredients in all New Age religions.

1. The world is what you think it is.
2. There are no limits; there is no separation between people and things because all is one; and anything is possible.
3. Energy flows where the attention goes.

4. Now is the moment of power. There is no power in the past or the future.

5. "Love" is "to be happy with," which is a direct translation of the word *Aloha.*

6. All power comes from within. Any apparent power that something else seems to have over you is illusory. You are giving it that power.

7. Effectiveness is the measure of truth.[13]

LYNN ANDREWS, THE BEVERLY HILLS SHAMANESS

Lynn Andrews, the author of such best-selling books as *Medicine Woman, Flight of the Seventh Moon, Jaguar Woman, Star Woman,* and *Crystal Woman,* is an attractive Beverly Hills shamaness who gives seminars called "Into the Crystal Dreamtime." As a female shaman, Lynn Andrews claims to be a member of the mysterious Sisterhood of the Shield, which is supposedly a group of forty-four women, each from different shamanistic cultures around the world.

In her "Into the Crystal Dreamtime" seminars Lynn Andrews guides her clients through "processes, ceremonies, and initiations to facilitate healing and personal growth." She uses crystals and other traditional tools used by shamans throughout the world to help free her clients. According to Andrews,

I have called these seminars "Crystal Initiations." And I use this name because I am going to have people use crystals to facilitate the focusing of energy. During the seminar they will gain much more clarity and beauty this way than they would if they did not use crystals. Also, when they go home they will have something tangible to work with.... They will be able to program those crystals with knowledge that they can use later on.[14]

Although Andrews has been accused by some of fabricating the existence of the Sisterhood of the Shield and her shamanistic journeys, she is a very popular speaker on the New Age lecture circuit. She uses shamanism to set people free from the limitations that bind them. Andrews said about her seminars:

The seminar has to do with getting at and giving up self-imposed concepts that create your fear and belief structures. I am particularly concerned with dealing with fear structures because fears are the rooting ground of our addictions. Addictions create holes in the etheric bodies, the etheric fields. Those holes are really where the life force leaks out of each and every one of us.... So you come to a teacher who is trained to be able to see you, and we can see where you leak that life force. We can see your addictions, and how you are misdirecting your heart, so to speak.[15]

As with other shamans and New Age teachers, Lynn Andrews addresses the problems of the human soul. Underneath all the shamanistic rhetoric we see an attempt to bring wholeness to the human personality. Wholeness which modern psychology, Valium, alcohol, escapism, and materialism have failed to bring. For underneath the pursuit of pleasure and materialism our generation is simply looking for answers.

The seduction of the New Age is that it promises to empower us for success in all aspects of our lives. There is something knit into the soul of every man and woman that wants to expand, grow, and become. Do Christians know that this is exactly what Jesus promised to those who enter the kingdom of God? The Bible teaches that God, the maker of all good things, will make perfect all who turn to him and worship him. What we see today is a massive wave of idolatry—worshiping idols of the New Age, deceptive gods raised up by the evil one to hinder man from receiving his highest good. When we begin to communicate biblical truth in its transforming power, we will see our world reached for Jesus Christ. The time has come for us to preach the same gospel that Jesus preached. As we do, the greatest revival in the history of mankind will take place.

A ONE-WAY TICKET TO PARADISE

There is a powerful driving force behind many of the spiritual, political, and social movements of our day: the deep inner need to return to Paradise. All men and women instinctively know in their hearts that they were created for a better world than this. We see this in the scientific and technological communities as they race to recreate our world. We see it in the Yuppie lifestyle where a new generation of Americans engage in the building of "cocoons" or "electronic wombs" through the purchase of big-screen televisions, video recorders, stereos, compact discs, computers, and satellite dish antennas.

Rock and roll groups like the Jefferson Starship sing songs

about leaving the planet in giant spaceships and building a new Utopia in the stars, while visionaries in NASA attempt to catapult mankind into the solar system. Movies like *2001: A Space Odyessy* and *2010,* based on science fiction author Arthur C. Clarke's novels, capture the public longing to become "star children." The New Age Movement has fanned the flames of this intense longing by creating events like Star Link 88, the brainchild of Diane Parrinello, who said in an interview in *Whole Life Times,* June 1988:

The event was initiated by a contact I had with extraterrestrials during the Harmonic Convergence on August 17, 1987 at Joshua Tree. [Joshua Tree is a national park where the New Agers gathered.] Prior to my experience at Joshua Tree I was not involved in anything metaphysical. I knew nothing about crystals. I knew nothing about visualization. . . .

. . . As we pulled into the entrance of Joshua Tree that's when I got the telepathic communication. It was: "You are being communicated to telepathically by extraterrestrials. We are the ones making the sound and we are the ones channeling the energies."[16]

Diane Parrinello received specific instructions from these "extraterrestrials" about creating an event called Star Link 88 at the Los Angeles Coliseum, and she stated that she has had numerous contacts with them. In the same interview she added, "Yes, it has continued since, and now it's not just the Pleiades. I have had contact from Sirius and also with a galactic group that claims to be from deep space." In addition, Diane claims she has had contact with beings from the "inner earth." "I would never have believed they were beings from the inner earth if I hadn't seen them myself. The heads of the ones I saw were very smooth-skinned except down at the center of the forehead where it looked like the back of a spoon. . . . They had a luminous skin color with a sort of greenish tone to it, but not quite."[17] Diane Parrinello claims to have been given a plan for the creation of the Star Link 88 event. An ad in *Conscious Living* reads:

On Saturday June 11, 1988, in the Los Angeles Coliseum, tens of thousands of people will be given the opportunity to activate the Power Vortex of Spiritual Energy that has lain dormant in the City of Angels for over two thousand years. There are places all over the earth where there is convergence of physical, magnetic and spiritual forces which are energy centers equivalent to chakras. Over the centuries, humanity has selected these points of convergence for temples, pyramids, and places of spiritual power, within the many electromagnetic, gravitational, geodetic and spiritual forces that circulate within the energy networks of the earth. There is a blueprint for the evolution of human intelligence—a crystalline etheric fabric which governs the human species. This fabric is made up of two distinct fields of vibration within the vastness of the planetary mind.

The first is the rainbow energy band which surrounds the planet and flows over the contours of the landscape, carrying specific patterns which determine the conscious programming of humanity during the next era of our evolution. The other, a deep earth biomagnetism, is sustained by underground veins of crystals which flow in organic pattern not unlike the veins and arteries of our own bodies touching every person and place on the planet.[18]

In case you dismiss this as "space cadet" talk left over from the mind-blown and brain-damaged 1960s, you need to realize that there is a growing movement which takes this kind of talk quite seriously and which is composed of scientists, medical doctors, movie stars, politicians, and military experts. This growing deception speaks to the deep need of man to fulfill his cosmic destiny. The true and living God has etched this destiny into the fabric of every person, but his ministers are not talking about it, and so the people are ripe for deception. Tragically, many preachers emphasize only the sinfulness of man and focus on God's judgment and on how evil unredeemed man is. In contrast, New Age activists talk about unleashing human potential and inhabiting the stars. It is true that mankind needs to repent. The Bible declares that human beings are clearly sinful, separated from God, and in need of the Savior who is Jesus Christ. This is absolutely true and it must be communicated intelligently and understandably to our generation. Many need to hear that foundational message. Jesus Christ told people that they needed to repent, but that was the *starting point* or the doorway into the "kingdom of heaven." Once you receive Jesus Christ as your personal Savior and have asked God to forgive your sins, then you have entered the kingdom of heaven and you must begin your spiritual journey, getting to know your Creator and the marvelous plan he has for your life. Yes, ongoing repentance is part of the plan, but don't forget that our God is a loving and forgiving God who wants us to know him intimately. He has wonderful things in store for us.

Is it any wonder young, intelligent people are seduced by the New Age? They look at the Christian church and they see little growth or creativity. No wonder they are ready to listen to the deceptions of the evil one.

Many Christians are like parents who have neglected to give their children the proper sexual education and who wake up to discover that their kids were learning the facts of life on the street. In a similar way, much of the church has not adequately communicated the truths of God's Word as it applies to the deepest longings of mankind. The living God has a majestic destiny for all who will come to him, a destiny that speaks to the deepest yearnings of the human heart. The Bible speaks of mankind's great destiny. As the apostle Paul said:

> But just as it is written, "Things which eye has not seen and ear has not heard, and which have not entered the heart of man, all that God has prepared for those who love him." (1 Cor 2:9)

> I pray that the eyes of your heart may be enlightened, so that you may know what is the hope of His calling, what are the riches of the glory of His inheritance in the saints, and what is the surpassing greatness of His power toward us who believe. . . . (Eph 1:18-19)

The God of the universe has something prepared for his

children which will totally eclipse Star Link 88. The apostle John gives us a brief description of what is to come:

> And I saw a new heaven and a new earth; for the first heaven and the first earth passed away, and there is no longer any sea. And I saw the holy city, new Jerusalem, coming down out of heaven from God, made ready as a bride adorned for her husband. And I heard a loud voice from the throne, saying "Behold, the tabernacle of God is among men, and He shall dwell among them, and they shall be His people, and God Himself shall be among them, and He shall wipe away every tear from their eyes; and there shall no longer be any death; there shall no longer be any mourning, or crying, or pain; the first things have passed away." (Rv 21:1-4)

The New Jerusalem is going to be a wonderful place, but Scripture gives us a clear warning that the unbelieving, the immoral, sorcerers, and idolaters, to name a few, are going to be thrown into "the lake that burns with fire and brimstone." This is a real and terrifying description of what it will feel like to be eternally separated from God. Understand that those who deliberately and consciously reject God will be there. The horrible consequences of turning from God and putting false gods in his place are spelled out very clearly in Scripture (see Revelation 21:27).

Jesus Christ is the Light of the world and he has given us his light. Before it is too late, we must "arise and shine." As the glory of the Lord fills our souls and our sanctuaries—the same glory that illumines the New Jerusalem—the nations and the peoples will come to the light. Kings, business executives, politicians, leaders, and everyone from all walks of life will come to the "brightness of your rising." Currently, our world is seeking counsel in the false light of the New Age. But this will change as the church of Jesus Christ opens to the glory of the Lord.

TWO

Overview of the New Age

T HE FIRST THING WE MUST UNDERSTAND about the New Age Movement is that it is not new. It is a compilation of old myths, of ancient Babylonian occult religions, Hinduism, and Buddhism, all dusted off and translated into high-tech Western scientific terms. What has been coined the New Age Movement by the mass media is really the combining and blending of various spiritual movements that are centuries old.

The origin of Hinduism dates back as early as 2000 to 1000 B.C. Hinduism has no historical founder, but its tradition teaches that its spiritual laws and truths were revealed to spiritual men called *rishis,* who lived along the banks of the Ganges and Indus rivers in northern India. According to Hinduism, *Brahman* is the supreme, absolute, eternal, infinite neuter Spirit-Being. *Brahman* is also perfect and unchangeable. Hinduism teaches that only that which is permanent is real. Because all things change except *Brahman,* only *Brahman* is real. Hundreds of other lesser gods can be worshiped by the Hindu because all gods are seen as different aspects of the one *Brahman.*

According to Hinduism, every living thing has a spirit or soul, called an *atman,* which comes from *Brahman.* The final destination of the human *atman* is union with *Brahman,* but this cannot be achieved in just one lifetime. Therefore, each individual *atman,* or soul, must pass from body to body, lifetime after lifetime, guided by the law of *karma.* This is called reincarnation, or the transmigration of the soul. The law of *karma* determines what type of life will be lived in each reincarnation. According to this law, your current life is the product of your deeds in past lives. Your *next* reincarnation will depend on your deeds during *this* life. It is this tenet which is the basis for many of the things taught by people like Shirley MacLaine, Ruth Montgomery, and various other gurus and spiritual teachers.

This belief in reincarnation has been given a fresh infusion of credibility by scientists like Raymond A. Moody Jr., M.D., author of *Life after Life,* which investigates NDEs (or Near Death Experiences) and OBEs (or Out of Body Experiences). Although not directly embracing reincarnation, his accounts of NDEs when one encounters a "Being of Light" paved the way for a New Age theology which openly accepts reincarnation. Moody reports that after meeting several "beings of light," the NDEer usually meets a supreme Being of Light, whom people with a Christian background often call God or Jesus but whom those of other religious traditions call Buddha or Allah. Still others apparently say that this supreme being of light is none of these personages, but nevertheless is someone very awesome. One wonders who this other being is. The Bible speaks about a Lucifer ("the shining one") who is a powerful spiritual being in rebellion against God. Could this "being of light" in reality be Lucifer?

According to Martha Knobloch, a Christian expert on the subject of reincarnation, powers of darkness can come as "beings of light" and create the hallucinations involved in NDEs and OBEs. In addition, Knobloch believes that demons can actually cause people to remember "past lives" that they never lived.

BUDDHISM

The religion of Buddhism was founded in India by Siddhartha Gautama (later called "the Buddha" or "enlightened one"), who lived between 560 and 480 B.C., as a protest against certain Hindu doctrines. Siddhartha Gautama was raised in an affluent family and did not even know that poverty existed until he left the pleasant confines of his father's palace. Siddartha was so disturbed by the poverty and despair that existed that he decided to go on a spiritual journey to find answers. Shaving his head and donning a robe, Siddhartha Gautama traveled and consulted with gurus and spiritual teachers. Finally, Siddhartha Gautama began to meditate, became "enlightened," and developed what became known as the Noble Eight-fold Path that would lead to *nirvana* or "perfect insight," a quality of mind. These eight techniques consisted of: (1) right belief, (2) right aspiration, (3) right speech, (4) right action, (5) right occupation, (6) right effort, (7) right thought, (8) right meditation.

In a nutshell, the Buddha's Noble Eight-fold Path is a program of self-effort that is designed to earn you peace.

Like every other New Age teaching and mystical practice, the road to Paradise is paved by your own personal spiritual performance. In other words, you earn your way to heaven through your works. This is the antithesis of God's method of salvation described in the Bible as based on faith in Jesus Christ. Ephesians 2:8-9 says, "For by grace you have been saved through faith; and that not of yourselves, it is a gift of God; not as a result of works, that no one should boast."

FROM THE PAST TO THE PRESENT

Coupled with these ancient belief systems (Hinduism and Buddhism) are the more recent ideas of women like Madame Blavatsky who founded the Theosophical Society and wrote *Isis Unveiled* in the late nineteenth century. Blavatsky's Theosophical Movement emphasized the Hindu and Buddhist teachings of reincarnation and taught there are *mahatmas* ("great souls" or exalted beings) who have come to earth to teach us the way to enlightenment.

The ideas of the Theosophical Society blended with Mary Baker Eddy's Christian Science teachings and with dozens of other hybrid religious movements in the early twentieth century. However, the most immediate spiritual predecessor of the contemporary New Age Movement was the Hippie movement of the 1960s and the earlier Beatnik movement of the 1950s. Both of these cultural and social phenomena came about as reactions to the materialism of the post-World War II years. Poets, writers, philosophers, and intellectuals (such as Alan Watts, Jack Kerouac, Allen Ginsberg, William Burroughs, and Gregory Corso) called for a new brand of American consciousness and popularized the use of marijuana and Eastern meditation in our culture. By the 1960s, the ideas of men like Timothy Leary were increasingly acceptable to larger segments of society, and the appeal of pop music groups, such as the Grateful Dead, the Jefferson Starship, the Doors, and the Beatles, ushered the psychedelic-mystical revolution into the living rooms of millions of ordinary middle-class teenagers. When John Lennon, Paul McCartney, Ringo Starr, and George Harrison began to follow the guru Maharishi Mahesh Yogi, the founder of Transcendental Meditation (TM), millions of Americans joined them.

Many of the spiritual movements now popular in the New Age Movement had their twentieth-century revivals in the 1960s and early 1970s. In fact, many social analysts believe that the New Age Movement is nothing more than an attempt to rediscover the interests of the 1960s and the idealism of the Hippie movement.

But the current New Age Movement has made some interesting departures from its earlier predecessors that reflect the maturity of its followers. There has been a de-emphasis in the use of drugs in favor of health foods, meditation, channeling, crystals, and astral projection. Channeling and astral projection have replaced the powerful pyschedelic experience of the 1960s, although there are signs of a possible resurgence of LSD through the work of modern shamanists like Terrence McKenna and the popularity of the Albert Hoffman Institute in Los Angeles, which seeks to protect the use of LSD experimentation. (Albert Hoffman was the Swiss chemist who accidentally discovered the chemical LSD.)

NEW AGE PRACTICES AND TERMS

To understand more clearly what the New Age Movement is we must understand some of the terms associated with it and the practices employed by it. We will see that some of them are distortions of Christian truth and of what should be part of a legitimate Christian lifestyle.

Channeling. The practice of channeling is not new. It is what the Old Testament termed mediumship, consulting with spirits, and spiritism. Channeling or mediumship is when an individual willfully yields to a spirit by going into a trance-like state. Channeling has been around for centuries and is mentioned in the Old Testament. King Saul consulted mediums and channelers when he was looking for supernatural answers. Instead of looking to God, he turned to the occult. First Samuel 28:7 says: "Then Saul said to his servants, 'Seek for me a woman who is a medium, that I may go to her and inquire of her.' And his servants said to him, 'Behold, there is a woman who is a medium at En-dor.'" We know that Saul knew it was wrong to consult mediums, for he had to visit the medium in disguise, having previously cut off all mediums and spiritists from the land. Because Saul was not in a right relationship with God at this time, he sought counsel from the channelers of his day.

Today there are several famous channelers: J.Z. Knight channels an entity or spirit called Ramtha, Jach Pursel mediums Lazaris, and there are thousands of lesser known channelers or mediums who give private consultations. Some even have their own television shows. In some cases, these channelers are fakes and charlatans, and in other cases they are actually letting spirits talk through them. The Bible is very specific about forbidding the practice of channeling, consulting spirits, or using mediums. Leviticus 19:31 states: "Do not turn to mediums or spiritists; do not seek them out to be defiled by them. I am the Lord your God." Leviticus 20:6, 27 says:

> As for the person who turns to mediums and spiritists, to play the harlot after them, I will also set My face against that person and will cut him off from among his people.... Now a man or a woman who is a medium or a spiritist shall surely be put to death. They shall be stoned with stones, their bloodguiltiness is upon them.

Shirley MacLaine, Kevin Ryerson, Jane Roberts, J.Z. Knight, Jach Pursel, and the thousands of others who are practicing and encouraging channeling may appear to be very compassionate and intelligent people. But the practices of channeling, consulting spirits, and mediumship are strongly condemned by God in the Bible.

Astrology. This New Age practice goes way back in ancient history. Although many of our country's newspapers regularly carry a horoscope column, it too is a practice specifically condemned by the Bible. The subject has enjoyed a new interest due to former First Lady Nancy Reagan's public disclosure of how she consulted the stars over major events involving former President Ronald Reagan. Nancy Reagan's astrologer turned out to be socialite Joan Quigley who has authored books on astrology such as *Astrology For Teens* and *Astrology For Adults.* Quigley said in a *Time* magazine story: "A horoscope can tell you more about yourself than a psychiatrist can tell you after many hours of consultations on his couch."[1] Other prominent astrologers include Jeane Dixon and Joyce Jillson; both have considerable media exposure and use detailed charts to "predict" future events.

Many Christians consider the consulting of horoscopes as harmless fun. But this is not the position that the Bible takes concerning astrology. The prophet Isaiah warns against the practice of astrology in Isaiah 47:13-14: "You are wearied with your many counsels; Let now the astrologers, Those who prophesy by the stars, Those who predict by the new moons, Stand up and save you from what will come upon you. Behold, they have become like stubble, Fire burns them; They cannot deliver themselves from the power of the flame. . . ." The prophet Isaiah warns the nation that they should seek God and not the stars or else destruction will come upon them.

Linda Goodman is one of the most famous astrologers of our era, selling over 60 million copies of her first two books on astrology, *Sun Signs* and *Love Signs*. Both of these books have been translated into over fifteen languages, and she has received bids of millions of dollars from publishing companies seeking the rights to her new books. Goodman is not a fatalistic astrologer who believes "it's all in the stars." Two themes emerge in her writing: (1) time does not really exist; and (2) when you learn to become a mover instead of a pawn, you rise above your horoscope. However, in an interview with *Whole Life Times* magazine Goodman responds to the question: "What do you think is going to happen in this New Age? You speak in one of your books about this being a time of preparation for the appearance of a Messiah." Goodman answers:

> I also point out in the "Lexigram" chapter of *Star Signs* that the Second Coming is not going to be a barefooted man floating down in a white robe. The Second Coming is in each heart, when each man and each woman realizes that "I too am a Messiah." And then I did a Lexigram on the word Messiah. I am he. She is me. He is her. I am she. He is me.[2]

This teaching totally opposes the biblical revelation of a personal God separate from his creation and is the direct antithesis of the incarnation of Jesus the Messiah. Astrology is not harmless fun. It is coupled with a philosophy contradictory to God's Word.

Crystals. If anything hallmarks the New Age Movement it is the use of crystals. I recently visited the Bodhi Tree Bookstore on Melrose Avenue in Los Angeles. This is the most famous New Age bookstore in the world, recently popularized by Shirley MacLaine in her television movie and book *Out on a Limb.* Inside the bookstore there was a large assortment of crystals for sale, as well as numerous books and magazines on the subject. Crystals are supposed to generate cosmic energy and facilitate higher consciousness and divine healing. Crystals have been used for everything from relieving depression to intensifying orgasms and warding off evil spirits. They are in a sense a New Age cure-all. Recently, a "Crystal Congress" was held in Los Angeles and noted speakers from around the world—like scientist and author Marc Vogel, Uma Silbey (jewelry designer and author), and Katrina Raphael (healing professional and author)—came to lecture on the healing arts and metaphysical applications of crystals, mineralogy, and geology.

The Bible does not specifically mention crystals. However, it is interesting to note that in Ezekiel 28:12-15 a reference to Satan appears. It reads: "Every precious stone was your covering." Could Satan use these objects of beauty to hide behind? There is nothing inherently wrong with crystals, and there is nothing wrong with owning them to enjoy their beauty. However, if a crystal has been used in conjunction with or as an instrument of mystical or occult practices, I strongly suggest that you get rid of it.

New Age Medicine and Holistic Health. New Age thinking has infiltrated the medical establishment and has begun to permeate the thinking of medical doctors. In this area it is difficult to discern between what are legitimate new forms of medicine based on Eastern medical techniques and new scientific discoveries, and what is clearly New Age or occult. Terms like homeopathy, herbs, chakras, acupuncture, deep tissue bodywork massage, rolfing, polarity energy balance, clinical ecology, environmental stress, Reichian Therapy, Tibetan Reiki Therapy, Kirlian photography, electroacupuncture, mineral balancing, chelation therapy, colon hydrotherapy, amino therapy, aromatherapy, integrated metabolic programs, bio-energetics, flower essences, and reflexology are just a few of the current trends in the medical arts.

When writer Norman Cousins was virtually able to cure himself of a fatal disease by watching old films of Laurel and Hardy, the Three Stooges, and the Marx Brothers, a whole new emphasis on the relationship between attitude and medicine emerged. This was followed by surgeon Bernard Siegel's best-seller *Love, Medicine, and Miracles.* Siegel suggests that "all disease is ultimately related to a lack of love, or to love that is only conditional, for the exhaustion of the immune system thus created leads to physical vulnerability."[3]

Many things about holistic health and New Age medicine are not only very beneficial and good for you but are also biblical. For instance, the Bible has many things to say about the relationship between attitude and health. "A tranquil heart is life to the body, But passion is rottenness to the bones" (Prv 14:30). "Pleasant words are a honeycomb, Sweet to the soul and healing to the bones" (Prv 16:24). "A joyful heart is good medicine, But a broken spirit dries up the bones" (Prv 17:22). It is clear that the relationship between attitude and health is a biblical concept.

There are aspects of holistic health and New Age medicine that are not compatible with Scripture. However, as Christians our energies should not primarily be directed toward denouncing New Age healing techniques but toward announcing our God's power to heal and transform. This doesn't mean that we are to be ignorant of practices which clearly violate the Scriptures. We need to steer ourselves and others away from holistic practices which specifically utilize Hindu and Buddhist philosophies regarding the use of energy or chakras or spiritism.

We should affirm an emphasis on nutrition. It is not New

Age to eat healthful foods free of chemical pollutants and dangerous pesticides. As Christians, we need to take care of our bodies. We should reduce our cholesterol intake by cutting down on red meats and fats, and eat more brans, fruits, and vegetables. This is not a subversive call to vegetarianism; it is scientific nutrition. Avoiding what is unhealthy does not mean that we are adopting the Hindu belief in vegetarianism and are afraid of eating our reincarnated ancestor. Scripture says: "Do you not know that your body is the temple of the Holy Spirit who is in you, whom you have from God, and that you are not your own? For you have been bought with a price: therefore glorify God in your body" (1 Cor 6:19-20).

In our misguided attempt to be purists for the faith we often miss the heartbeat of God, which is to heal people. This does not mean that we are to allow false doctrine to spread but that we are to be agents of God's healing power. Luke 9:1-2 says, "And he called the twelve together, and gave them power and authority over all the demons, and to heal diseases. And he sent them out to proclaim the kingdom of God, and to perform healing." Also, when Jesus Christ commissioned his disciples he said, "They will lay hands on the sick, and they will recover" (Mk 16:18).

As Christians we can miss the point that God loves people with a passion and that he wants to heal them. If I were a sick nonbeliever and went for help to Christians who did not believe that God heals the sick today and who wouldn't pray for me, in my desperation I would turn to anything else that promised hope and health. I might dance naked under a full moon, shout *OM*, and gargle with Tibetan swamp water if I thought it would help. Wouldn't you? Finger-pointing and theological circumspection seems pretty pathetic when you are face-to-face with a sick person. The church is to be in the business of healing in the name of Jesus Christ. The problem really isn't the New Age Movement, the problem is unbelief and disobedience in the church. "Is anyone among you sick? Let him call for the elders of the church, and let them pray over him, anointing him with oil in the name of the Lord; and the prayer offered in faith will restore the one who is sick, and the Lord will raise him up" (Jas 5:14-15).

Healing services led by the elders of the church should be part of the life of every church, whether evangelical, fundamentalist, or charismatic. Individual Christians should pray for the sick on a regular basis. The Gospels command us to minister in Jesus' name. Sometimes we will see miracles. Other times God might use doctors and medicine or even choose not to heal. Whatever the case, we are called to bring all ills and troubles to him, confident that he will deliver us in his time.

Meditation. This ancient Hindu and Buddhist practice involves emptying the conscious mind in order to become passive and to awaken the God-consciousness within you through the use of a mantra. By concentrating and chanting a mantra word, your mind supposedly becomes attuned to what mystics call your higher self or cosmic consciousness.

Meditation is an integral part of most New Age practices, but there is a radical difference between prayer and New Age meditation. Prayer is communication with God through Jesus Christ. It may involve verbal prayer or "praying in the Spirit," but this communication is always directed toward the person of God. New Age meditation, on the other hand, is an emptying process where one focuses on a mantra which is usually a chant designed to contact a Hindu deity or demon. Eastern meditation involves the "dropping of your guard" and the relinquishing of the control of your rational mind, thus opening you to the realm of the demonic. For you are opening your mind to the spiritual realm but you are not focusing on God, and therefore other spirits can communicate with you.

There is a long tradition of sound Christian meditation, not to be confused with Eastern forms of meditation. It is certainly proper to meditate on the Word of God or to think in a concentrated matter about what God is doing in your life. "I have more insight than all my teachers, For thy testimonies are my meditation," says the writer of Psalm 119:99. Meditation on the Bible involves focused thinking about what God has said. It is completely different from opening your mind to the "cosmic consciousness."

Christians need to be wary of Christian ministers and authors who teach non-biblical meditation and other exercises which are based on Eastern mysticism. When Christians who are not open to the supernatural power of God and praying in the Holy Spirit feel an emptiness in their souls they can be tempted to explore Eastern meditation and philosophy cloaked in Christian terminology.

Visualization. First of all, visualization to some degree is a normal function and creative tool of the mind. Every person before beginning any project or goal employs some kind of visualization in order to achieve it. Many athletes use a technique of visualization when they mentally picture themselves winning or performing a specific task successfully. Studies show that good automobile drivers who have low accident records often visualize or fantasize how they would get out of a particular accident situation while they drive. When they are faced with a potential accident, they have already rehearsed in their minds what action they are going to take to avoid it.

A certain degree of visualization is necessary to perform activities in life successfully. This kind of visualization is, however, significantly different from the shamanistic Hinduism of someone like Shakti Gawain, guru and author of *Creative Visualization*, who employs the technique of visualization in the mystical or occult sense. In this type of visualization, your mind or mind power becomes the god or source of all power. You begin to believe that you can control everything in your life through visualizing it. The result is that you begin to play God and attempt to control everything through visualization. Instead of praying to God and worshiping him, you begin to spend all your time visualizing your success, your healing, your dreams. God gets crowded out of the picture entirely. Visualization then violates the commandment, "You shall have no other gods before Me" (Ex 20:3).

There are two equally dangerous errors that can be made here. The first is to fail to understand that there is a biblical principle of learning how to see through the eyes of faith and learning how to see ourselves as God sees us. This is beautifully illustrated in the story of Elisha when the prophet says, "'O Lord, I pray, open his eyes that he may see.' And the Lord opened the servant's eyes, and he saw; and behold, the mountain was full of horses and chariots of fire around Elisha" (2 Kgs 6:17). Here we see that God opened a person's eyes to see the true nature of the spiritual battle all around them and the fact that the armies of God were on their side in the invisible realm, even though the situation looked bleak in the physical world.

However, this brings us to the second error we can make: failing to understand the difference between seeing through the eyes of faith and using visualization as a form of mind power, believing you can have, be, or do anything to which you direct the power of your mind. This practice is reminiscent of Adam and Eve's fatal pride when they listened to the serpent's promise, "You will be like God" (Gn 3:5). To substitute mind power or visualization for the genuine power of God is to fall for the age-old deception that started all our trouble.

The Bible as one good spiritual guide among many. New Age members all make the mistake of viewing the Bible as just another "spiritual guidebook" among many other equally valid ones. However, the Bible is the only Word of God. The apostle Paul says, "All scripture is inspired by God and profitable for teaching, for reproof, for correction, for training in righteousness" (2 Tm 3:16). Hebrews 4:12 says, "For the word of God is living and active and sharper than any two-edged sword, piercing as far as the division of soul and spirit, of both joints and marrow, and able to judge the thoughts and intentions of the heart."

HOW NEW AGE DECEPTION
MANIFESTS ITSELF IN THOUGHT LIFE

It is equally important that we fully understand some of the New Age ideas so we can protect ourselves and others from them. The following is a summary of beliefs commonly held by Eastern religions and the New Age Movement. Some of these ideas have found their way into the church, corporate America, and society as a whole.

Everything that happens to you—good and bad—you created. The idea that you are totally responsible for your own reality is a dangerous one, based on half-truths. It places enormous guilt and psychological stress upon people. It is true that God has given us the power of free will. Our choices help to create reality. But God has also created the universe to abide by laws, and as a consequence of obeying certain principles, we can protect ourselves from evil and manifest blessing and prosperity.

It is true that nonChristians can prosper, be in good health, and avoid "bad" things by following God-given principles. But this is not the same as telling people that whatever happens in their lives was caused or created by them. There are people in the New Age who teach that the Jews brought the Holocaust on themselves, or that when a woman is raped she subconsciously brought it into her life. There are those who believe that people are born in ghettos because they chose this for themselves, and that we are responsible for our own sicknesses and tragedies. This type of thinking is really a terrible form of bondage.

Try to imagine the psychological bondage that occurs when a person suffers a devastating accident and they must continually ask themselves, "How did I create this?" We live in a fallen world with evil forces that are sometimes out of our control, and in this fallen world there is going to be painful suffering that we did not directly create.

Some in the church believe that by right confession and faith we can avoid every problem. The "name it and claim it" practice exalts our own desires and reduces God to our personal butler in the sky. We will not be immune from every problem in life, but we do have a loving and all-powerful God who in his time promises to work everything to our good.

There is no such thing as evil. Many in the New Age and Eastern mystical religions do not believe in evil or a personal devil. They believe instead that both good and bad, positive and negative, darkness and light, or God and the Devil are parts of the same cosmic whole. This is the Eastern view of duality, and it is very dangerous because it encourages passivity in the face of evil. Totalitarian governments, crime, and violence are seen merely as expressions of *karma* and are therefore not actively resisted.

We see this kind of moral passivity toward evil emerging in the Christian church when people take Romans 8:28 out of context: "And we know that God causes all things to work together for good to those who love God, to those who are called according to his purpose." That doesn't mean that everything that happens to us is the will of God. It means that he will redeem everything that happens to us as we put on the full armor of God, resist the Devil, and stand in the promises of God. The Christian is not supposed to be passive; we are not just to "go with the flow." Passivity instead of personal and spiritual responsibility is not the biblical way. We are more than conquerors in Christ Jesus, and that means we are going to have to do some fighting! For the Christian, evil is real and we are actively to resist it and fight it.

We are all God. A basic premise in New Age thinking is that each of us is a god. The true purpose of all meditation is to awaken the god-consciousness inside of us. This error reminds us again of the serpent's temptations, "You will be like God, knowing good and evil" (Gn 3:5). In Isaiah 14:12-15 the prophet Isaiah tells the story of Lucifer, the star of the morning whose greatest sin was pride and the desire to be God. In this passage of Scripture we see that five different times Satan says in his heart "I will"—the complete opposite of what Jesus Christ taught us to pray in the Lord's prayer— "Thy will be done." Jesus did not come to do his own will but the will of the Father.

Our past lives influence our present lives. The idea that this lifetime is only one in a series of incarnations comes from the Hindu religion. The Bible teaches that there is only one life on earth, and after death we are judged. The idea of reincarnation is not only false but it also eliminates the necessity of salvation by faith in Christ, because in this view of things you earn your way to heaven gradually by working off your sins through successive lifetimes.

Soul mates. The New Age idea of soul mates complements the theory of reincarnation. Basically, soul mates are people whose lives are intertwined for the purpose of working out their *karma* together. Thus a man and a woman who are powerfully attracted to each other romantically and spiritually are called to live together for the purpose of working out their cosmic destiny. This view has been popularized by people like author Richard Bach who wrote *Jonathan Livingston Seagull* and psychics who have appeared on TV talk shows. In reality this concept creates havoc in many people's lives because men and women have left their husbands and wives for another, believing that their marriage was a mistake and their cosmic destiny is to join with their new-found soul mate.

In contrast, while the Bible teaches that a man and woman can become one for a sacred and special spiritual purpose, this divine union is discovered through a lifetime commitment, hard work, prayer, and fidelity as well as romance and eroticism. A married man and woman in Jesus Christ have embarked on a marvelous cosmic adventure through life. They do not desert each other every time they are attracted to a member of the opposite sex. As mature spiritual people, they recognize the difference between attraction and true love. God's plan builds a life of faithfulness, trust, and joy, while the myth of soul mates only produces moral anarchy and broken hearts.

There are many roads to God. Many people today believe that you can get to heaven or reach union with "the universal life force" by following Buddha, Jesus, your guru, or any one of the thousands of paths offered. This philosophy is inherent in New Age thinking, which views Jesus as merely an "enlightened teacher" or a spiritual master. However, in John 14:6 Jesus says, "I am the way, and the truth, and the life; no one comes to the Father, but through Me." Jesus wasn't trying to be a cosmic dictator; he was simply telling the truth. It is only Jesus Christ who effectively deals with the root problem separating man and God in the first place—sin. Jesus Christ was the only one who destroyed the power of sin and death on the cross. All the other spiritual teachers circumvented sin and merely applied first aid to the root problem.

There is no personal God, only cosmic consciousness. People involved in the New Age and Eastern mysticism believe in the concept of God. However, their definition of God is quite different than the Judeo-Christian view of a personal, living God of the universe who expressed himself in Jesus Christ. The god of the New Age is an ambiguous energy force or cosmic consciousness of which everyone is automatically part. Their view is that we are all "God" collectively; thus, we have god-consciousness. I have read hundreds of different definitions of this New Age god and it is obvious that there is no real consensus. In reality, the god of the New Age is no god at all. It is a mythological creation based on Hinduistic, Buddhist, and Eastern mystical principles. Even Buddha called this god "perfect nothingness"—the opposite of a loving heavenly Father who sent his Son to die for his creation and who loves each one of us intimately. This non-personal energy force is a hollow illusion that can only bring despair. Who would want to trade a Savior who died for us and who called us his friends for "perfect nothingness"?

MOVING INTO THE FUTURE

Clearly, the major premise of the spiritual search embodied in the New Age Movement is that man can be god. The Devil's sales pitch to our ancestors was remarkably similar to what we hear the gurus and New Age pitchmen telling their prospective followers today when they offer revelation, cosmic consciousness, ancient wisdom, and secret knowledge. It is the forbidden fruit all over again, and it ultimately brings imprisonment rather than enlightenment.

Technological innovations are brewing a whole new wave of consciousness-altering activities that are about to explode on the American scene like drugs did in the 1960s and channeling did in the 1980s. The new technology of the "mind machine" is offering psychedelic, consciousness-altering, and intelligence-increasing adventures in inner-space. Michael Hutchison, author of the definitive book on mind-machine technology, *Megabrain*, outlines how machines that evolved from the biofeedback devices of the 1960s can now electronically alleviate pain, cure diseases, produce sleep states, improve creativity, increase intelligence, raise I.Q.s, and stimulate people into states of higher consciousness. Some of the mind machines now available on the market include the Synchro-Energizer, the D.A.V.I.D. 1, the MC^2, the Alpha Stim, the RelaxPak, and The Graham Potentializer; these devices will do for the user what drugs, meditation, and other mystical practices are now doing. Add to this whole new array of technology such things as psychoactive designer foods which can change your consciousness through nutrition, and it becomes obvious that the entire New Age Movement is on the verge of taking a quantum leap into the future.

WHY THE NEW AGE MOVEMENT EXISTS

One day I walked into a popular health food store in Coldwater Canyon in Los Angeles, and everywhere I looked I saw beautiful wood shelves stocked with luscious and colorful displays of vitamins, nutrients, herbs, spices, healthy-looking and vibrant tomatoes, apples, oranges, green bell peppers, bananas, mangoes, avocados and the like. The meat and fish section was well stocked with organically bred steaks, shrimps, sausages, and other foods. There was a special health food bakery section with pies, cakes, desserts made with natural honey, whole wheat, and fruits. The magazine racks were filled with books on diet, health, meditation, and the New Age. The employees were cheerful and upbeat. Customers looked between the ages of twenty and forty-five years old and were attractive and confident.

The reason for this store's spectacular success and growth is because it meets the needs of the people. The owners of this store are in touch with the people and know how to reach them. The New Age Movement itself is a lot like that health food store in Coldwater Canyon. It prospers and spreads because it addresses the needs of the people and communicates its ideas in a contemporary and understandable manner to the culture. The New Age has become synonymous with all that is healthy and positive.

In their best-selling book *A Passion for Excellence: The Leadership Difference,* authors Tom Peters and Nancy Austin write about what makes certain companies successful and what makes others fail. One of the principles discovered by the authors as they researched hundreds of the top corporations of the United States was that successful companies know how to listen to the public. Companies that fail are out of touch with the needs of people. The authors cite an example of one successful company's exercise designed to force them to stay in touch with their public. Employees fill out an index card called "A Daily Dose of Reality" as they phone customers and find out if they were happy with their service. The objective is threefold: (1) to let customers know they are important to the company; (2) to uncover problems before they become major irritants; (3) to give management a daily reminder of where the real world is—with the field reps and customers.[4]

Obviously the church of Jesus Christ is not corporate America, nor do we need to run the church like a business or a corporation. The church of Jesus Christ is a living body of believers empowered by the Holy Spirit. But that does not mean that we cannot learn from corporate America and the business world. The Book of Proverbs says:

Wisdom shouts in the street,
She lifts her voice in the square;
At the head of the noisy streets she cries out;
At the entrance of the gates in the city, she utters her sayings:
How long, O naive ones, will you love simplicity?
And scoffers delight themselves in scoffing, And fools hate knowledge?
Turn to my reproof,
Behold, I will pour out my spirit on you;
I will make my words known to you. (Prv 1:20-23)

Is the church really out on the streets listening to the pain and anguish of our present generation? Like the corporations who are out of touch, are we presuming to know but acting out of ignorance? Must we be so surprised that we are failing?

Many Christians do not have any idea to what extent the New Age Movement has spread among young people who have rejected Christianity. Christianity in America is often out of touch with what is really going on in our society, and this is reflected in the style and content of our ministries. "Church" is often not much more than a ritual which involves choir robes, pews, ushers, pulpits, and lots of standing up and sitting down.

I am not suggesting that churches should not have rituals or order in worship. Obviously structure and ceremony are part of ministry. But sometimes they hinder what God wants to do. There are times when the rituals of the church get in the way of the life of Jesus Christ. Many young people are not alienated by Jesus Christ or the Bible but by rituals they see as meaningless. For them, the style and structure of middle-class Christianity is an obstacle between them and Jesus Christ. They choose to go to gurus because they feel that New Age worship is more akin to the vitality of their own spirituality.

In an effort to expose the deception of New Age teaching, some Christian ministers and authors go overboard and insinuate that everything connected with the New Age Movement is demonic and related to a massive global conspiracy of the Anti-Christ. This simply is not true. Excessive paranoia erodes the credibility of those who make such a claim and reduces their effectiveness in ministering to people involved in the New Age. There are many rational, intelligent, loving, sincere, and gifted people who would view themselves as somehow connected to the New Age Movement, in that they are involved in meditation, consciousness raising, yoga, Eastern mysticism, and the like. To imply that all of these people are "demon possessed" or following the Antichrist reflects a real poverty of Christ's love and a superficial spirituality. In an article in *New Realities* (June 1988), David Spangler, a leader in the New Age Movement, president of the Lorian Association, and author of the book *Emergence: The Rebirth of the Sacred,* had this to say about the movement:

> Therefore, for those of us who profess belief in a New Age, it is important to understand that the New Age is essentially a symbol representing the human heart and intellect in partnership with God, building a better world that can celebrate values of community, wholeness, and sacredness. It is a symbol for the emergence of social behavior based on a worldview that stimulates creativity, discipline, abundance, and wholeness.... It has very little to do with the emergence of psychic phenomena.

> The New Age has little to do with prophecy or the imaging of a new world but everything to do with the imagination to see our world in new ways that can empower us toward compassionate, transformative actions and attitudes. If we remember this, then we can forget the New Age of channels, crystals and charisma and get on with discovering and co-creating a harmonious world that will nourish and empower all of us on this planet and all our children who will be the inheritors of the future.

> The New Age is often seen as a time of individual empowerment, and New Age literature is filled with books on how to claim one's divinity, to proclaim "I am

God!" and be more creative, abundant, happy, prosperous and spiritual. Personal empowerment is important, but the essence of the New Age is the expression of compassionate love and social awareness and responsibility that reaches beyond the self to embrace and empower others.[5]

THE NEW AGE'S BASIC ERROR

We see in David Spangler's words a desire for many things that could be Christian. His view reflects many in the New Age Movement. One starts from the philosophical position that man is good and that this goodness, if allowed to emerge, will guide us to a new world order of harmony and peace. However, the reality of history shouts war, bloodshed, revolution, and chaos because man is a sinner and in need of true salvation. This does not mean that man cannot do good, beautiful, and godlike things, for man was created in the image of God and has many of his attributes. However, since the Fall sin has been at work in the world, and that is why such positions of optimism always end in destruction when they are separated from a truly biblical worldview.

In the eighteenth century, philosopher Jean-Jacques Rousseau believed that if man is good by nature, it follows that he stays good as long as nothing foreign to him corrupts him. Thus the myth of the "noble savage" and the belief that it is environment that corrupts mankind. In the nineteenth century, Karl Marx formulated the view that mankind's problems are the result of a giant class struggle between the "haves" and "have nots" and once this basic economic conflict is resolved global harmony will result.

The Hippie movement of the 1960s started with peace, love, and unity and ended with heroin overdoses, Charles Manson, and the violent Weathermen Underground. Recent Marxist revolutions, such as that in Cuba under Fidel Castro, have resulted in oppression, despair, and bloodshed far more widespread than that practiced by the government they revolted against.

THE CHRISTIAN CHALLENGE

When Christians throw stones at those involved in the New Age Movement, they only reinforce the prejudices against Christianity. What is needed is loving, compassionate communication with real answers, not glib cliches and hollow talk about the devil. The people in the New Age have a social agenda built upon a philosophical foundation. Simply telling them to repent, without offering them an equally inspiring, compassionate, and philosophically sound alternative, is counterproductive. People in the New Age are for the most part sincere, and they need honest and intelligent answers. They need to understand how the Bible speaks to their personal issues and to the broader issues of our day. The majority of these people have been preached at, but they have not had the person of Jesus Christ truly communicated to them. As a result, they have sought answers in the New Age Movement and in its activities. Instinctively they know we live in a supernatural universe and so they look to channelers, psychics, and clairvoyants for supernatural answers to questions the church should be addressing, but is not.

For example, Kevin Ryerson is one of the nation's best-known channelers. Ryerson goes into a trance and allows "entities" from another dimension to speak through him. In February of 1987 at the Whole Life Expo in Pasadena, California, over 3,000 people came to hear Ryerson channel one specific entity who is supposed to be a 2,000-year-old metaphysician who was part of the Essene community during the time of Christ. Ryerson says,

> My channeling is modeled after the Edgar Cayce readings. A person can ask very direct inquiries of the sources that speak through me and they can receive information that they can use as a supplement in the decision-making process. . . . People ask questions about occupational direction, health and well-being, and personal relationships much as one might ask from other serious disciplines, such as occupational therapists, a psychologist, or a person skilled in the holistic healing arts. It all comes up in one package and it is called trance channeling.[6]

When we hear these words our reaction should not only be to think of demon possession. We should hear the cry of people who are so desperate for answers in life that they will try anything—crystals, channeling, astrology, and psychics. People are hurting and are looking for a way out of their pain. If such a person went to your local church, would he hear the gospel of Jesus Christ or a humanistic theological interpretation of the Bible? If he did hear the gospel, would it be only John 3:16 and the message of salvation over and over again every Sunday? It is true people need to hear the message of salvation, but they also need answers. And the

Bible contains thousands of scriptures besides John 3:16—scriptures that pertain to careers, guidance, love, sex, money, clothing, shelter, business, and peace. Tragically, not enough churches communicate the full range of the gospel of the kingdom that Jesus Christ preached.

Have we as Christians taken the time and commitment to allow our own lives to be transformed by the wide spectrum of biblical truth? Without that first step of transformation and empowerment in our own lives, we will be tragically ineffective in our efforts to reach those in the New Age Movement.

THREE

Spiritual Gifts and Supernatural Power

CHRISTIANITY IS THE SUPERNATURAL EXPRESSION of a living relationship with Jesus Christ. It is not a set of rituals and religious ceremonies that center around Sunday morning—although that may be an important part of it. Spiritual gifts are an essential part of the normal operating procedure of true biblical Christianity. The authentic New Testament church of today and the future cannot choose to accept or reject spiritual gifts. God has not given the church that option.

In 1 Corinthians 12:1 the apostle Paul has this to say about the use of spiritual gifts: "Now concerning spiritual gifts, brethren, I do not want you to be unaware (ignorant)." It is clear that understanding and using spiritual gifts is not supposed to be a mystery. The gifts of the Holy Spirit are powerful tools in fulfilling the ministry that Jesus Christ has given the church. They are instruments for doing good and healing all who are oppressed by the devil. Parts of the contemporary church have rejected the use of spiritual gifts and as a result have often found themselves unable to be the full expression of Jesus Christ upon this planet. In some cases, the church has adopted the tools of modern psychology and behaviorism as substitutes for the power of the Holy Spirit.

The result is that often Christians treat human ills with secular psychotherapy couched in Christian words, instead of relying on the Holy Spirit to give fresh revelation, healing, and deliverance to the many problems besetting contemporary society. Ironically, while many segments of the church deny the reality of the supernatural in favor of humanistic explanations based on the philosophy of scientific materialism, the New Age Movement flourishes all around the church by offering satanic counterfeits of the gifts of the Holy Spirit. While much of the church suppresses the supernatural dimension of Christianity, an entire generation of highly educated men and women who were indoctrinated in the philosophy of secular humanism and scientific materialism have rejected those ideologies in favor of an Eastern mystical worldview which affirms the reality of the supernatural. The bottom line is that these spiritually hungry people understand the limitations of human intelligence in solving problems and providing answers. This is why astrology, psychics, channelers, shamans, mystics, Satanists, mediums, and visionaries of the New Age have become so popular.

It is clear that many people today have a tremendous hunger for supernatural revelation, wisdom, and guidance—a hunger that I believe was placed there by the Creator and which is being exploited by New Age practitioners. People are flocking to mediums and channelers because a large segment of the Christian church denies that supernatural communication with God is possible. However, this posture of unbelief was not the position of the first-century church. 1 Corinthians 12:1-5 says:

> Now concerning spiritual gifts, bretheren, I do not want you to be unaware. You know that when you were pagans, you were led astray to the dumb idols, however you were led. Therefore I make known to you, that no one speaking by the Spirit of God says, "Jesus is accursed"; and no one can say, "Jesus is Lord," except by the Holy Spirit. Now there are varieties of gifts, but the same Spirit. And there are varieties of ministries, and the same Lord.

It is clear from these passages that God designed the church to be a supernatural church. When Paul says, "Now concerning spiritual gifts, bretheren, I do not want you to be unaware," he means exactly what he says, and yet we find large portions of the church totally ignorant of these things. The spiritual gifts are not nice little toys to play with but the spiritual equipment necessary to heal and guide people through life. People are paying large sums of money to seek out trance channelers so that they can find supernatural power to make their lives work. Ironically, this supernatural power is what God has already given to the church.

THE SLEAZE FACTOR

Unfortunately, there is a small but visible number of ministries which exercise the gifts of the Holy Spirit without integrity. I call this syndrome the "sleaze factor," when people abuse the gifts of the Holy Spirit. Many things can be done in the name of the Holy Spirit that have nothing to do with him. Some services become like circus shows with a lot of emotionalism being passed off as the "anointing." You see it when ministers try to work up the audience emotionally. You see it in so-called revivals where the evangelist knows how to manipulate the audience. This lack of integrity has done a great deal to discredit the genuine movement of the Holy Spirit, who is a person of order and peace and whose actions are always full of grace.

UNDERSTANDING THE GIFTS OF THE HOLY SPIRIT

It is important to understand that the practice of spiritual gifts is not an attempt to compete with the New Age by offering our own Christian array of supernatural displays. The key issue here is that the New Age correctly surmises that we live in a spiritual universe, and it attempts to bring supernatural power to bear on the problems of the material world. If you analyze many of the things going on in the New Age Movement, you will see counterfeits of the Holy Spirit's work. In order to have a counterfeit, you must first have an original. The gifts of the Holy Spirit are the "originals" given to us by God to give the church supernatural tools for ministry.

The gifts of the Holy Spirit are not mysterious or complicated. Tongues, prophecy, healing, miracles, discerning spirits, and interpreting tongues should be natural for the church. When Christians are abiding in the Word of God and open to the power of the Holy Spirit, these gifts should be in operation. Paul writes in 1 Corinthians 12:4-11:

Now there are varieties of gifts, but the same Spirit. And there are varieties of ministries, and the same Lord. And there are varieties of effects, but the same God who works all things in all persons. But to each one is given the manifestation of the Spirit for the common good. For to one is given the word of wisdom through the Spirit, and to another the word of knowledge according to the same Spirit; to another faith by the same Spirit, and to another gifts of healing by the one Spirit, and to another the effecting of miracles, and to another prophecy, and to another the distinguishing of spirits, to another various kinds of tongues, and to another the interpretation of tongues. But one and the same Spirit works all these things, distributing to each one individually just as He wills.

According to the Bible the gifts of the Holy Spirit should operate throughout the body of Christ. These gifts are the tools that God has given us to minister effectively to people. They are our surgical instruments for operating on a lost and dying world.

CAUTIONS CONCERNING SPIRITUAL GIFTS

The Bible is clear regarding such issues as prophecy: "But know this first of all, that no prophecy of Scripture is a matter of one's own interpretation, for no prophecy was ever made by an act of human will, but men moved by the Holy Spirit spoke from God" (2 Pt 1:20-21). All prophecy must be judged or evaluated in light of what Scripture says. If someone gives a prophecy that is in contradiction to anything the Bible says, then we must judge that prophecy as false. The Word of God is our safeguard against deception, and Christians must be discerning.

Paul gives clear guidelines for the use of spiritual gifts:

> What is the outcome then, brethren? When you assemble, each one has a psalm, has a teaching, has a revelation, has a tongue, has an interpretation. Let all things be done for edification. If anyone speaks in a tongue, it should be by two or at the most three, and each in turn, and let one interpret; but if there is no interpreter, let him keep silent in the church; and let him speak to himself and to God. And let two or three prophets speak, and let the others pass judgment. (1 Cor 14:26-29)

Spiritual gifts are to benefit us, but they must be used according to specific guidelines. Paul assumes that the church will use spiritual gifts. His issue of concern is their *correct* usage. First, we see that the purpose of the spiritual gifts is to "edify" or build up. We need to be wary of ministries which do nothing but tear down. There is a place for admonishment and correction, but the minister or prophet must give leadership and direction, not just correction. Second, Paul says "let the others pass judgment" on the prophecy given. When we hear a word of prophecy we are to evaluate it based on the Scripture. There will never be a prophecy from God that changes Scripture or goes beyond what Scripture teaches by inventing a new doctrine.

We need to be wary of prophecies which make the Holy Spirit inside of us uncomfortable. The peace of God, acting as an umpire in our hearts, will guide us. If that peace is disturbed or if we feel uncomfortable, then we need to listen to this warning from the Holy Spirit. Furthermore, we must study the Word of God so that we know firsthand what the Bible says. "Be diligent to present yourself approved to God as a workman who does not need to be ashamed, handling accurately the word of truth" (2 Tm 2:15).

Another important principle can be found in 1 Corinthians 14:32-33, where Paul says, "And the spirits of prophets are subject to prophets; for God is not a God of confusion but of peace, as in all the churches of the saints." All things are to be done decently and in order. People who interrupt services with emotional displays are not moving in the Spirit of God. The gifts of the Holy Spirit are to be used in a proper manner.

GREATER WORKS THAN THESE

As we have stated earlier, the current New Age Movement and the revival in Eastern mysticism and the occult is in reality a collective cry for help from a lost generation that has not seen the reality of the power of God demonstrated with integrity. The solution to this problem is the ministry of the New Testament church, with its total reliance on Jesus Christ and on the accompanying power of the Holy Spirit, reaching the culture of our day.

This is to be the ministry of the church today and of every

individual Christian: "Truly, truly, I say to you, he who believes in Me, the works that I do shall he do also; and greater works than these shall he do; because I go to the Father" (Jn 14:12). The church and the individual Christian should be doing the very same works that Jesus Christ did while he was on the earth, as well as the "greater works than these."

What were the works of Jesus Christ? First of all "he went about doing good, and healing all who were oppressed by the devil." In addition, "God anointed him with the Holy Spirit and with power" (Acts 10:38). It is clear that the essential prerequisite for the church and the individual Christian is that we are to be anointed with the Holy Spirit and with power before we can go about doing good and healing all who are oppressed by the devil.

Therefore before we look at how we can go about doing good and healing all who are oppressed, we must examine how we are to receive the power that Jesus Christ talked about—the power which was the driving force behind the New Testament church as outlined in the book of Acts. In Acts 1:8 Jesus Christ says to his disciples before they turned their world upside down: "But you shall receive power when the Holy Spirit has come upon you; and you shall be my witnesses both in Jerusalem, and in all Judea and Samaria, and even to the remotest part of the earth" (Acts 1:8).

The early disciples did not simply charge madly into the world after hearing the words of the Lord Jesus. To do so would have meant certain failure. They needed to receive supernatural power from heaven before they could fulfill their ministry. The individual Christian and the church as a whole is like an automobile that needs gasoline; it is absolutely useless without this important fuel, no matter how fine the engine is or how talented the Christian is. Neither the automobile, the Christian, nor the church can go anywhere without the fuel. For the church and the Christian, this fuel is the Holy Spirit.

In many cases, the church has attempted to fulfill the commission of Jesus Christ without the power of the Holy Spirit. Thus the contemporary church in many quarters has relied on human effort, the machinery of the flesh. But without the power of the Holy Spirit the individual Christian and the church can do little of lasting consequence. The words of Jesus Christ are not idle words: "And behold, I am sending for the promise of My Father upon you; but you are to stay in the city until you are clothed with power from on high" (Lk 24:49). Every believer in Jesus Christ must be "clothed with power from on high" before he or she can effectively preach the gospel to the people involved in the New Age.

HOW TO RECEIVE POWER FROM ON HIGH

"Receiving power from on high" is not a mysterious or mystical thing. Jesus said, "For John baptized with water, but you shall be baptized with the Holy Spirit not many days from now" (Acts 1:5). This was fulfilled when the disciples were meeting in an upper room on the day of Pentecost. Acts 2:1-4 says:

And when the day of Pentecost had come, they were all together in one place. And suddenly there came from heaven a noise like a violent, rushing wind, and it filled the whole house where they were sitting. And there appeared to them tongues as of fire distributing themselves, and they rested on each one of them. And they were all filled with the Holy Spirit and began to speak with other tongues, as the Spirit was giving them utterance.

As I have talked with people all over the country I have found fear and misunderstanding regarding what is called the "baptism of the Holy Spirit." I believe that the reason for this is that the Enemy will attempt to do anything he can to stop God's people from receiving the power they need to live the victorious Christian life and to fulfill the ministry to which Jesus Christ has called us.

First of all, it is a fact that there have been millions of Christians throughout history who have not accepted the idea of being baptized in the Holy Spirit and speaking in tongues. Yet these mighty saints of God have been faithful to pray, intercede, and evangelize the world. However, this does not contradict the fact that it is impossible for a Christian or a church to be effective for Christ without the Holy Spirit. For without exception every effective Christian throughout history has acknowledged the absolute necessity of living by the power of the Holy Spirit, being led by the Holy Spirit, and being filled daily by the Holy Spirit. The key issue here is not what term is used—being "filled with" the Holy Spirit or being "baptized in" the Holy Spirit. The key issue is that each of us needs to rely totally on the power of God's Spirit to live our Christian lives. Even if one believes in what is called the baptism of the Holy Spirit, it is a tragic mistake to assume that this infilling with the Holy Spirit is a one-time experience. For although there may be a particular moment in time when an individual recognizes that he or she received the Holy Spirit, we should seek more of the Lord's energy and strength every day, every moment. John Wesley felt his "heart being strangely warmed" and Charles Finney experienced "overwhelming baptisms." But in every case, every great man and woman of God throughout history knew firsthand the importance of the power of the Holy Spirit.

ONE MAN'S PERSONAL EXPERIENCE

Since I had no Christian upbringing and was raised primarily as a secular humanist, I had few religious preconceptions. To me, either Jesus Christ was the resurrected Messiah and *everything* in the Bible was true, or he was not raised from the dead, in which case *none* of the Bible was true.

As someone deeply involved in Eastern mysticism, the New Age, and altered states of consciousness for almost a decade, I had regularly experienced all kinds of spiritual phenomena, such as mental telepathy, communicating with spirit guides, blissful states, supernatural power, and occult powers. Although I had been raised in a secular humanistic household which embraced the philosophies of scientific materialism and existentialism, I had rejected these ideologies as spiritually bankrupt in favor of the spiritual reality offered by the Eastern religions and the New Age. I had personally entered a spiritual reality that was denied by many in our Western culture, as well as by many in the Christian community.

When I surveyed much of Christianity during my spiritual pilgrimage I noticed that it was not the same kind of church that Jesus Christ talked about or that the Bible spoke of. In other words, I reasoned to myself that if Christianity was really true then the Christian churches would be like the churches in the Book of Acts and that God would still be performing miracles through the lives of Christians. I reasoned that if Jesus was who he claimed to be and if Christians who claimed to possess the truth really had the truth, then there would be some kind of supernatural evidence. I surmised that if Christianity was born in the miraculous, if Jesus Christ performed all kinds of extraordinary miracles during his earthly ministry, and if the apostles performed miracles, then this flow of miracles would not have come to a screeching halt in the twentieth century just when it was needed most. Either the miracles never happened at all or they happened then and would have to happen now.

However, when I attended churches I did not see any evidence of the reality of Jesus Christ's resurrection in their midst. There was no joy or miracles in these congregations. All I saw was the Christian "religion" of standing up and sitting down, of choir robes, ceremony, steeples, and boredom. If this homogenized mass of middle-class values and religious words was Christianity, I wanted nothing to do with it. Either Christianity was true or it wasn't, and if it was true then Jesus Christ had to work miracles in the lives of his followers today.

CONFRONTING THE SUPERNATURAL GOD

My prejudices against Christianity were shaken on the campus of the University of Missouri where I was studying psychology and taking a number of courses relating to a brand new field of study entitled "Altered States of Consciousness." As part of our college curriculum we studied the teachings of gurus, Carlos Casteneda, and Eastern disciplines from a psychological perspective.

For my personal amusement I would debate Christians in philosophy class and usually win when attempting to disprove the claims of Jesus Christ on intellectual grounds. However, about this time I ran into what was then called the "Jesus Movement." Here were young men and women just like myself, many who had been part of the Hippie movement in California and who had been involved in drugs and Eastern mysticism. At first I wasn't particularly impressed as I met this ragtag legion carrying Bibles and quoting scriptures. However, some of these Bible-believing Christians were not the buffoons the media made them out to be, and they challenged me to rethink my position and to read books by men like Dr. Francis Schaeffer. I was shocked to find out that it was possible to be a Christian and to be an intellectual at the same time. Furthermore, these Christians believed in miracles, in answered prayer, and in speaking in tongues. I saw miracles occur as lives were instantly transformed and people were delivered from drugs and alcohol immediately after prayer. These Christians were not practicing the stiff, country-club Christianity I had seen in the past. They were bold and communicated with authority and confidence. In addition, they prayed about everything and seemed to delight in worshiping God in song and in the Spirit. When I prayed with them I experienced personally the living presence of Jesus in a profound, intimate, and unmistakable way. All of my preconceptions and prejudices regarding Christianity were shaken by the presence of the living Jesus.

After accepting Jesus into my life, I felt the call of the Holy Spirit to seek more from him. For me this was not a theological issue for I had regularly been experiencing supernatural phenomena for years. Now that I was a Christian I seemed to be involved in an intense spiritual conflict with unseen powers of darkness and temptations towards drugs, sex, and alcohol that were very strong. I do not think it is possible to live the lifestyle I lived and then exit from it unharmed. There is a supernatural dimension to this way of life, and I think what is needed is a distinct severing from its forms of bondage. In addition, I believe that there must be a powerful infusion of the life force of the Holy Spirit into the human personality in order for a person to progress in the kingdom of God. There are so many forces at work in our culture which have spiritual dimensions (such as child abuse, alcoholism, depression, suicide, drugs, homosexuality, disease, poverty, personality disorders, low self-esteem, lust, and hatred—to name a few). Sometimes these physical and emotional conditions are connected to the unseen reality or spiritual dimension, and in order for wholeness and positive change to occur there must be a corresponding change in the spiritual dimension. One way to facilitate this positive change is to receive power from on high or to be baptized in the Holy Spirit.

Pastor Carl Valente of the Lamb's Club Ministries in New York City counseled me privately about being baptized in the Holy Spirit. He encouraged me to pray and fast about this matter. Several days later, Reverend Valente and I met in the library of the Lamb's Club in New York City; he "laid hands" on me and prayed for me to receive the Holy Spirit. As he was praying and we were praising God, I felt the presence of Jesus Christ fill the room. I saw what seemed to be a vision of myself kneeling at his feet. Tears ran down my face. When I found myself in the presence of Jesus, my response was simply to fall at his feet and worship him. His love poured through me and cleansed me. His power and presence surged through me, and I felt totally accepted and loved by him. I left the room feeling indescribably invigorated, as if a burning torch was lit in my heart. Since then, through all the seasons of my spiritual life, this flame of the Spirit has never ceased to burn within me. From then on I had a stronger desire to read the Word of God and a new sense of spiritual power. For me, being baptized in the Holy Spirit was not the beginning of a primrose path to heaven with no obstacles, challenges, or temptations. My Christian experience has been exceedingly difficult, with all kinds of trials, disasters, and danger. Being baptized in the Spirit is not a "cure-all," but it is a tremendous source of power and strength.

Some Christians have had a more calm and subdued experience than I did. I know of one individual who knew he was baptized in the Holy Spirit when he began to laugh with delight, while others have simply felt a quiet but deepening sense of God's presence. We serve a unique and creative God who interacts with each one of us in different ways. The key is that we need to be open to his dealings in our lives.

THE DEVIL AND PSYCHOLOGICAL BONDAGE

Another aspect of the supernatural power available to the church is in the area of spiritual warfare against our spiritual enemies. Ephesians 6:11-12 says: "Put on the whole armor of God, that you may be able to stand against the schemes of the devil. For our struggle is not against flesh and blood, but against the rulers, against the powers, against the world forces of this darkness, against the spiritual forces of wickedness in the heavenly places."

Modern psychology and much of contemporary Christianity ignore the reality of a personal Devil and demons. Very few churches practice the supernatural ministry that Jesus outlined when he said, "Cast out demons." In fact, Jesus specifically said, "And as you go, preach, saying, 'The kingdom of heaven is at hand.' Heal the sick, raise the dead, cleanse the lepers, cast out demons. . . ." (Mt 10:7-8). Jesus spent a great deal of time casting out demons and taking authority over unclean spirits; however, the contemporary Christian church usually ignores Jesus' example and plain commands. In contrast, the New Age Movement teaches its followers to open themselves quite freely to spirits from other dimensions. We have a disobedient church wary of the reality of the supernatural, while those in the New Age Movement regularly practice supernatural power.

It is crucial that we understand the supernatural element

to all inner healing and that demons and the Devil are very much a part of psychological problems. The Gospels have numerous references to Jesus encountering people who were possessed or oppressed by the Devil. That does not mean we should see demons everywhere we go or that we should attribute every psychological problem to the demonic, but it does mean we should have the same awareness that Jesus had concerning the reality of evil in people's lives. I have personally encountered numerous individuals who have been bound by demonic influences. Alcoholics, drug users, and people involved in the occult and New Age are especially susceptible to the influence of demons. Even Christians who are filled with the Holy Spirit can be oppressed by demonic powers.

There is a spiritual dimension to alcoholism, drug addiction, pornography, homosexuality, and occultism. Fortunately, Jesus promises supernatural deliverance to anyone who is bound by them. He gave every believer full authority to bind the power of the devil in people's lives.

GOD WANTS YOU TO ENJOY LIFE

People all over the world want to enjoy life. This is what the American dream is all about—having a home, a family, and money for things that make life pleasurable. To reach a new generation of Americans, we must communicate that God affirms abundant life. Too often Christians promote a negative lifestyle of limitations, restrictions, and rules. Nobody in their right mind would be interested in this kind of life, and it emphatically is not what the Bible teaches.

The New Age and humanistic psychology have been successful in winning adherents and making an impact on our culture because they make positive statements about life. Young, thinking, and creative people who have goals and ambitions flock to these disciplines because they offer "tools" to release their full human potential and to "empower" them for achievement and success. The back cover of Anthony Robbins' book *Unlimited Power: The Way to Peak Personal Achievement* says:

> It's not about power over other people. It's about power over yourself! Yes, you can do, have, achieve, and create anything you want out of life. Anthony Robbins has proved it. Robbins, the undisputed master of the magic of mind power, shows you in these pages how to harness yours. He demonstrates—passionately and eloquently—that whatever you think will be, that your state of mind determines what you can do and can't do, and that all successful results can be modeled and duplicated. His enthusiasm is contagious as he shows you how to reprogram your mind in minutes to eliminate fears and phobias; fuel your body with spectacular health and energy; dramatically improve your interpersonal relationships; become a persuasive communicator and create instant rapport with anyone you meet; use the success of others to remodel yourself; discover the five keys to wealth and happiness; master the ultimate success formula.[1]

Mr. Robbins conducts seminars around the world for professional athletes, politicians, Fortune 500 executives, and housewives. He also conducts the Tony Robbins

Firewalk Seminar where people who have mastered their minds walk over red-hot fiery coals.

Sometimes Christians can focus excessively on being broken and humble, believing that their present state of failure, depression, and poverty is God's will for them. Although Jesus does talk about the seed of corn dying in the ground and about the way to life through the cross, he does not call us to wallow in weakness, depression, and failure. He calls us to believe that he has wonderful plans for us. As we surrender to him, he gives us a vision of life beyond our limitations. His power, wisdom, and love is ours if we walk in his ways. In him we are freed from sin and death. Anthony Robbins cannot offer us eternal life with our great and glorious Creator.

MASTER THE POSSIBILITIES

In the final analysis, Christians have the only message of true liberation. Only the Bible can "unlock human potential." In the very beginning of creation God gave mankind dominion over the planet. Connected to the Spirit of the living God we can have the powerful, creative inspiration necessary to recreate our lives and society. We have the "mind of Christ" and should be coming up with answers to the hunger crisis, pollution, and other ills of our world. God did not call us to stand on the outside of society and complain about how bad everything is. We are to take leadership. Men and women empowered by the Holy Spirit can give sane, practical, creative, and supernatural solutions to the challenges facing our culture. When the children of Israel were pursued by Pharaoh and his chariots, Moses in the power of God divided the Red Sea. Now the chariots of nuclear annihilation, hunger, crime, AIDS, drugs, and war are upon us. But the children of God in the power of the Holy Spirit can give answers in the midst of crisis. This means taking first-century supernatural power and translating it into the language of our day. God exists now, is talking now, is working miracles now, and we must enter the "now" with supernatural authority.

LOVE: THE HIGHEST GIFT AND GREATEST POWER

All around us in our society are alienated, fragmented, lonely, and hurting people. Feminists, Marxists, homosexuals, New Agers, mystics, Muslims, Freudians, and atheists do not arrive at their philosophical positions as much from logic as from emotion. Underneath the fabric of all the rhetoric is a whole sea of pain, hurt, rejection, and awkward attempts to find love, joy, and acceptance.

We need to understand that the vast majority of the people involved in the New Age Movement are there because of deep emotional pain. Many of them have experienced the stifling rigidity, legalism, and lovelessness of a Christianity that was devoid of the real love of Jesus Christ.

Beneath the crystals, astral trips, and channeled entities are people who are starving for the embrace of Jesus as he says, "I love you and I accept you." However, since Jesus ascended into heaven and sent his Holy Spirit upon the church, we as the church must go in Christ's name and in his love embracing people and calling them out of their sin and into new life in him.

When I became a Christian, it was not logic and reason which won me to Christ, although they had their place. It was the love of Jesus Christ that I felt through the lives of caring Christians which brought me to the Father. My life was one of tremendous inner pain until the love of Jesus Christ touched me. Although I had a million different intellectual reasons for my involvement in radical politics, psychedelic drugs, and New Age mysticism, the energizing force that drove me into experimentation with things like cosmic consciousness, the teachings of Baba Ram Dass, meditation, astral projection, mental telepathy, Zen, yoga, and the like was my inner emptiness.

When we hear the angry rhetoric of a radical feminist, a militant gay, or a New Age activist we must learn how to get beyond their anger and listen to their hurt. People enter ashrams, follow gurus, attempt to leave their body, visit channelers, and join religious movements because they hurt. Many of these people are crying out for the touch of Jesus Christ in their lives, but all they see is the machinery of religion.

If these people do not sense our love and commitment to them as people whom Jesus Christ died for, we will make no real, effective penetration into our post-Christian culture. Real love expresses itself in finding ways to communicate to this world and build bridges between Jesus and the people he died for. If we really love our neighbors, we will talk to them in their language and reach out to them in love.

The Christians who led me to Jesus befriended me. They spent hours with me, loving me unconditionally. These Christians would invite me to their homes for meals and take me on picnics where the love and grace of the Holy Spirit was evident. In my heart, I knew these people were

Christians not by their rhetoric, slogans, or Bible verses but because of their love. These Christians loved each other and they loved me, and my hard and angry heart could not help but melt.

Jesus Christ was able to embrace me because these Christians freely gave of themselves. In total contrast to the radicals and hippies I knew who talked endlessly about love and peace but remained selfish and self-centered, these Christians expressed to me the heart of Jesus. In their eyes I saw him; in their words I heard him. Through them Jesus Christ stepped into my life, and for the first time I found real food to satisfy my hunger. Through their hands the Bread of Life was extended to me.

This authentic New Testament Christianity was totally different from the nonpersonal mysticism I had been practicing. I had spent hours in yoga meditation, chanting *OM*, doing psychedelic drugs, and having supernatural experiences. Even the serenity and mystical peace I achieved through meditation seemed cold and illusory compared to the magnificent reality of knowing the liberating love of Jesus Christ.

Long hours of theological discussion did not win me to Christ. Love did. Love was the one thing I did not experience in all my New Age journeys and the only thing I was really looking for.

FOUR

Multi-Dimensional Warfare

ACCORDING TO THE BIBLE, there is multi-dimensional spiritual warfare occurring on earth. Life is far more than getting up in the morning, going to work, and going to sleep. Dr. Francis Schaeffer comments on this spiritual warfare in his book *The Great Evangelical Disaster*:

But the Scriptures make clear that we as Bible-believing Christians are locked in a battle of cosmic proportions. It is a life-and-death struggle over the minds and souls of men for all eternity, but it is equally a life-and-death struggle over life on this earth. On one level this is a spiritual battle which is being fought in the heavenlies. Paul's letter to the Ephesians presents the classic expression: "For our struggle is not against flesh and blood, but against the rulers, against the powers, against the world forces of this darkness, against the spiritual forces of wickedness in the heavenly places" (Eph 6:12).

Do we really believe that we are engaged in a cosmic battle? Do we really believe that there are "world forces of this darkness" which rule our age? Or as the Apostle John says, do we really believe that "the whole world lies in the power of the evil one" (1 Jn 5:19)? If we do not believe these things (and we must say that much of the evangelical world acts as if it does not believe these things), we certainly cannot expect to have much success in fighting the battle. Why has the Christian ethos in our culture been squandered? Why do we have so little impact upon the world today? Is it not because we have not taken the primary battle seriously?[1]

Dr. Schaeffer raises the key point which Christians must consider. Do we believe that there is a war between the forces of good and evil, fought in the visible *and* invisible realm? Do we understand that depression, lust, addiction, fear, poverty, and sickness can have spiritual overtones? Do we realize that involvement in the New Age Movement or Eastern mysticism can open the door to the dominion of evil spirits in one's personal life? Everything in life has a spiritual dimension to it, for the spiritual reality exists as a parallel reality to the physical one that we perceive with our physical senses.

BLINDED BY THE LIGHT

There are many people in our world who cannot see the truth of God in Jesus Christ or understand the reality of God's existence because they have been blinded by a dazzling and deceiving light of the evil one. The apostle Paul says in 2 Corinthians 4:3-4:

> And even if our gospel is veiled, it is veiled to those who are perishing, in whose case the god of this world has blinded the minds of the unbelieving, that they might not see the light of the gospel of the glory of Christ, who is the image of God.

Secular humanism and New Age occult philosophies have kept many people from seeing the glorious light of Jesus Christ. Can you imagine looking at the Son of God in all his resurrected splendor and not recognizing who he is? Salvation is like sitting in a cold and dark cave, and someone comes in with a blazing torch and leads you out to safety.

Imagine being trapped inside a burning building. Some people inside the building are saying there is nothing wrong, that everything is as it is supposed to be. Yet you feel the heat and smell the smoke and hear the fire engines outside. You run to the window and see the firemen holding a net and shouting "Jump! Jump!" You turn around and see someone sitting at a table, eating dinner and smiling. In a second you realize that if you stay you are going to burn to death. You realize that the person sitting at the dinner table while the building is burning down is crazy! You plead with him to jump, but he replies, "Relax! There's nothing wrong; we have always had fires." Then there is an explosion, and heat and flames rush through the door; you jump to safety just in time.

Many people are in exactly the same state of mind as the person eating dinner in the burning building. They are deceived by sin and totally unaware of its life-destroying force. Even Christians are anesthetized to the seriousness of man's plight. The church of Jesus Christ must begin to intercede for those in peril that they might see the light. We are not to hate them because they are blind. We must go to battle for them.

THE NEW AGE VIEW OF EVIL

The Bible is quite clear that there is a spiritual battle going on in this world between the kingdom of God and the kingdom of Satan. However, the New Age Movement, Eastern mysticism, and secular humanism do not believe that there exists an evil force at work in the universe. In fact, the New Age sees good and evil merely as complementary or balancing forces—the *yin* and the *yang,* parts of the same whole. True historical evil is simply seen as illusion.

Nikos Kazantzakis, the author of *Zorba the Greek* and *The Last Temptation of Christ,* wrote about his view of evil in his book *Report to Greco* when commenting on the effect that Friedrich Nietzsche's philosophy had upon him. His views closely parallel the progression that the New Age Movement and society in general has taken concerning evil:

Although I did not have this consciously in mind at all, the two figures, Christ and Anti-Christ, gradually merged. Was it true then, that these two were not eternal enemies, that Lucifer was not God's adversary? In the course of time, as I studied the work of this prophet [Nietzsche] opposed to God, I mounted step by step to a foolhardy, mystical unity. The first step of initiation, I said, was this: good and evil are enemies. The second step was: good and evil are fellow workers. The highest step, the highest I was able to reach at present, was good and evil are identical![2]

This is precisely what the New Age and many people influenced by Eastern mysticism believe. For them there is no good and bad—only duality, two halves of the great cosmic whole. Concepts like light and darkness, positive and negative, pain and pleasure are all seen as a duality. Christian concepts concerning an absolute truth and a real struggle between God and the Devil simply do not exist.

Psychiatrist M. Scott Peck, author of the best-sellers *The Road Less Traveled* and *People of the Lie,* courageously embarked on an honest examination of the nature of evil, a task few modern scientists have undertaken. Peck, who left Buddhism for Christianity, found that as he was embracing Christianity he had to confront the subject of evil. After witnessing two exorcisms, Peck realized that demons and the Devil do exist. *Omni* magazine describes Peck's book:

People of the Lie describes evil characters that Peck has experienced in his psychiatric practice and whose presence he fears in politics and on TV. The evil are attracted to power and can often be spotted by expression and gesture. Defining Satan as "a real spirit of unreality," Peck fears that our government to a considerable extent is pervaded and operates by a real spirit of unreality. It is descending into unreality.[3]

THE BIBLICAL VIEW OF EVIL

Whereas the New Age Movement and secular society have distanced themselves from the Judeo-Christian concept of the struggle between heaven and hell, Scripture maps out a very specific strategy that evil has for the human race and how spiritual deception is an integral part of it. In Revelation 12:7-9, John gives us an account of the battle that is going on in the invisible realm:

And there was a war in heaven, Michael and his angels waging war with the dragon. And the dragon and his angels waged war, and they were not strong enough, and there was no longer a place found for them in heaven. And the great dragon was thrown down, the serpent of old who is called the devil and Satan, who deceives the whole world; he was thrown down to the earth, and his angels were thrown down with him.

The Bible is clear that the direct expression of this spiritual war is deception. What exactly is the nature of this deception? Satan lies to mankind about reality. He tries to undermine the truth of God's existence and character, salvation in Jesus Christ, even his own existence.

As we have seen in 2 Corinthians 4:3-4, the apostle Paul unravels more of the mystery behind this satanic conspiracy to deceive mankind: "And even if our gospel is veiled, it is veiled to those who are perishing, in whose case the *god of this world has blinded the minds of the unbelieving,* that they might not see the light of the gospel of the glory of Christ, who is the image of God." Paul states that they have been blinded by the "god of this world." Who is the "god of this world"? He is Satan (or Lucifer, which means the "shining one"). Lucifer hinders people from seeing the gospel by blinding them with his shining lies. It is no accident that many people involved in Eastern mysticism have seen what is termed "the great white light." As a former practitioner of Eastern mysticism, I saw this light, and it was not Jesus.

Spiritual deception is a direct expression of the spiritual conflict between God and Satan. In 2 Corinthians 11:13-15 the apostle Paul warns that this spiritual deception can occur even in the church:

> For such men are false apostles, deceitful workers, disguising themselves as apostles of Christ. And no wonder, for even Satan disguises himself as an angel of light. Therefore it is not surprising if his servants also disguise themselves as servants of righteousness; whose end shall be according to their deeds.

When we hear the detailed and supposedly scientific accounts of angels, beings of light, spirit guides, and entities communicating with man, we need to be able to discern whether or not they are from God. The key is to align these accounts with the truth of Scripture. John warns us to use discernment concerning spirits:

> Beloved, do not believe every spirit, but test the spirits to see whether they are from God; because many false prophets have gone out into the world. By this you know

the Spirit of God: every spirit that confesses that Jesus Christ has come in the flesh is from God; and every spirit that does not confess Jesus is not from God; and this is the spirit of the Anti-Christ, of which you have heard that it is coming, and is now already in the world. (1 Jn 4:1-3)

Jesus warned us about the role of deception in the great war between Himself and the devil: "And Jesus answered and said to them, 'See to it that no one misleads you. For many will come in my name, saying, "I am the Christ," and will mislead many'" (Mt 24:4-5). Further on in the same passage of scripture, Jesus continues, "And many false prophets will arise, and will mislead many" (Mt 24:11). Finally, Jesus warns them a third time:

Then if any one says to you, "Behold, here is the Christ," or "There he is" do not believe him. For false Christs and false prophets will arise and will show great signs and wonders, so as to mislead, if possible, even the elect. Behold, I have told you in advance. If therefore they say to you, "Behold, he is in the wilderness," do not go forth, or, "Behold, he is in the inner rooms," do not believe them. For just as the lightning comes from the east, and flashes even to the west, so shall the coming of the Son of Man be. (Mt 24:23-27)

In the great cosmic battle for mankind, Satan will raise up false prophets and false Christs to deceive people. Spiritual deception is part of his military strategy, and we must not be ignorant of his ways.

FALSE PROPHETS AND A DIFFERENT GOSPEL

In this multi-dimensional spiritual conflict, Satan shows a profound understanding of human psychology. He knows our strengths and weaknesses and understands how we tick better than any psychologist or modern behaviorist.

With this in mind Paul writes:

But I am afraid, lest as the serpent deceived Eve by his craftiness, your minds should be led astray from the simplicity and purity of devotion to Christ. For if one comes and preaches another Jesus whom we have not preached, or you receive a different spirit which you have not received, or a different gospel which you have not accepted, you bear this beautifully. (2 Cor 11:3-4)

Paul warns of the danger of receiving a "different gospel." Since the gospel of Jesus Christ is essentially a message that men and women can be saved through faith in Jesus Christ, a different gospel would be anything which attempts to change the simple message of devotion to Christ.

In the Book of Galatians Paul warns again about a different gospel: "But even though we, or an angel from heaven, should preach to you a gospel contrary to that which we have preached to you, let him be accursed. As we have said before, so I say again now, if any man is preaching to you a gospel contrary to that which you have received, let him be accursed" (Gal 1:8-9). There are a number of false religions, cults, and New Age groups which claim to have received a revelation from an angel, spirit guide, entity, or even aliens from another planet. Paul warned us centuries ago to steer clear of these beings who are bringing a different gospel other than the one Jesus Christ preached. We must be aware that even within the church there will be those who will attempt to preach a different gospel. One of our strongest defenses is a thorough and complete knowledge of the Bible. It is imperative that Christians diligently study the Bible.

THE ANTICHRIST AND HIS ROLE IN DECEPTION

In 1 John 2:18 and 22, the apostle John writes: "Children, it is the last hour; and just as you heard that antichrist is coming, even now many antichrists have arisen; from this we know that it is the last hour.... Who is the liar but the one who denies that Jesus is the Christ? This is the antichrist, the one who denies the Father and the Son."

As we examine many of the current teachers in the higher consciousness and New Age Movements, we see an alarming number of them who are denying that Jesus is the Christ. It is unclear whether they are denying him out of ignorance or out of willful rebellion, but it is clear that a spirit of deception is at work.

Part of Satan's strategy to woo people into worshiping him rather than God is the use of false signs and wonders. Satan counterfeits the miracles of God in order to get people to follow him. "And he performs great signs, so that he even makes fire come down out of heaven to the earth in the presence of men." "And he deceives those who dwell on the earth because of the signs which it was given him to perform in the presence of the beast, telling those who dwell on the earth to make an image of the beast who had the wound of the sword and has come to life" (Rv 13:13-14). Here we see that Satan will not only use miraculous signs to deceive people but that he will also counterfeit the resurrection.

Behind all the miracles and signs performed by the beast is a strategy designed to solicit the worship of men, for the driving force behind the Devil is a desire to be God. Worship is powerful. It is a means of establishing a supernatural relationship. It focuses the energy and devotion of human beings and it brings about a communion with the object that is worshiped. It is no accident that God is restoring worship to the church and that Satan desires to subvert that worship for himself. Just as true worship to God releases God's people to enter dimensions that they have never known before, so the worship of Satan releases the power of evil in a way that we do not yet fully understand.

There are powerful spiritual laws at work in the universe that revolve around the principle of worship. Satan exposes his hand to us when in the beginning of Jesus Christ's earthly ministry he comes to Jesus asking him to worship him in exchange for his earthly kingdoms: "Again, the devil took Him to a very high mountain, and showed Him all the kingdoms of the world, and their glory; and he said to Him, 'All these things will I give You, if You fall down and worship me' " (Mt 4:8-9).

The kingdoms of the world are in Satan's possession temporarily and so the Devil had the legal right to offer them to Jesus. Worship is vitally important to Satan because he would have given up all his earthly kingdoms if Jesus would have worshiped him. It is not surprising then that all New

Age teachings and Eastern mystical and occult practices involve the concept of worship. These religious systems which supposedly teach that man is the center of the universe and is his own god practice worship of some kind of leader or god. For example, transcendental meditation begins with a ceremony where fruit is offered in a form of worship to an ancient guru. Here within the context of this supposed science of transcendental meditation we see a ceremony of Hindu worship.

THE ANTI-CHRIST AND "ONE WORLD" CONSPIRACIES

It is with a certain amount of reluctance that I delve into the area of the Anti-Christ as the driving force behind the idea of one world government. However, I believe it is important to understand the spirit of the Anti-Christ and how it relates to current world affairs.

As I have already stated, I do not believe that the New Age Movement or certain political movements are all part of one large satanic conspiracy. This interpretation ignores the fact that there are millions of people involved in New Age activities because they are honestly attempting to find truth, and in their exposure to Christianity they have come up against something which has too often been shallow, legalistic, and non-biblical. It is true that there are satanic forces at work in the New Age—just as there are satanic forces at work in the church.

But there is a very real spirit of the Anti-Christ at work in our world who has direct influence upon political, religious, and economic movements. Both Christians and New Agers must be aware of the fact that they can be pawns in a game they do not fully understand. Let us not forget that Adolph Hitler was supported by some Christians because he stood for morality and disguised himself as Christian. In the same way, a new dictator rising from the political right or left would have the capacity to seduce both Christians and New Agers by speaking the words they want to hear. Even in the recent presidential political race we saw master political strategists push the public's "hot buttons." But there is a vast difference between actual substance and the mere repetition of words.

In the next decade we are going to see the New Age Movement become a more political force as it continues to merge with nuclear disarmament, ecology, world peace, one world government, education, and multi-national corporations. As Christians have become a major political force, so the New Age Movement will enter into a new era of political activism.

THE CHALLENGE FOR THE CHURCH

Are we ready to engage in this cosmic battle? Are we fully clothed with all the weapons which God has made available to us in order to pull down strongholds of deception and bondage? Are we actively interceding for the people who are blind to the danger they are in by their involvement in New Age activities? Are we strong from the spiritual nourishment of the Holy Spirit as we boldly expose the presence and works of Satan? Are we able to bring, in Jesus' name, release from bondage to those who are trapped, emotionally and psychologically? These are some of the challenges the church is facing today, and to meet these challenges we need not only the awareness of the problem and the knowledge of the solution, but also the *authority* to engage the two. In Matthew 16:18-19, Jesus says:

> And I also say to you that you are Peter, and upon this rock I will build My church; and the gates of Hades [Hell] shall not overpower it. I will give you the keys of the kingdom of heaven; and whatever you shall bind on earth shall be bound in heaven, and whatever you shall loose on earth shall be loosed in heaven.

Jesus clearly says that the church should be like a great heavenly battering ram smashing down the gates of hell and freeing the captives inside. Jesus has given us supernatural power to take authority over the New Age Movement. You and I have been given the keys of the kingdom and the power to bind New Age, occult, and demonic activity in the name of Jesus Christ.

FIVE

Taking Authority over the New Age

L IFE IS NOT JUST WHAT WE SEE with our eyes. There is an entire universe beyond the realm of our senses, and it is in this world that many of the watershed events of life really take place. Part of the reason that there is such an intense fascination with horror and the occult in our generation is a subconscious attempt to explore the spiritual dimension, the existence of which is ignored or denigrated by many of the sophisticated segments of our society.

In Ephesians 6:10-18, Paul outlines the complexity of the spiritual combat we are all involved in:

Finally, be strong in the Lord, and in the strength of his might. Put on the full armor of God, that you may be able to stand firm against the schemes of the devil. For our struggle is not against flesh and blood, but against the rulers, against the powers, against the world forces of this darkness, against the spiritual forces of wickedness in the heavenly places. Therefore, take up the full armor of God, that you may be able to resist in the evil day, and having done everything, to stand firm. Stand firm, therefore, having girded your loins with truth, and having put on the breastplate of righteousness, and having shod your feet with the preparation of the gospel of peace; in addition to all, taking up the shield of faith with which you will be able to extinguish all the flaming missiles of the evil one. And take the helmet of salvation, and the sword of the Spirit, which is the word of God. With all prayer and at all times in the Spirit, and with this in view, be on the alert with all perseverance and petition for all saints. (Eph 6:10-18)

In fact, the Greek word for principalities, *arche,* denotes an organized spiritual army with rank and order. The Greek word for powers is *exousa,* which means superhuman potentate or literally a superhuman who wields controlling power. Who is this superhuman? It is the Devil or Satan—the enemy of God and mankind. The words "the rulers of darkness" come from the Greek word *kosmokrator* which translates "a world ruler," an epithet of Satan. The apostle Paul says that we are in mortal combat with the armies of hell in the spiritual realm, and this combat has real consequences in the physical realm.

Francis Schaeffer comments about this battle in his book *The Great Evangelical Disaster:*

The primary battle is a spiritual battle in the heavenlies. But, this does not mean, therefore, that the battle we are in is other worldly or outside of human history. It is a real spiritual battle, but it is equally a battle here on earth in our own country, our communities, our places of work and our schools, and even our own homes. The spiritual battle has its counterpart in the visible world, in the minds of men and women, and in every area of human culture. In the realm of space and time the heavenly battle is fought on the stage of human history.[1]

In the areas of politics, theology, sexuality, art, literature, film, music, culture, law, science, medicine, and business a spiritual conflict rages. This is not a form of Christian mysticism or a wild trip into the world of demonology. It is a mature Christian perspective which understands the responsibility for intercession and action.

BINDING THE STRONG MAN

And He was casting out a demon, and it was dumb; and it came about that when the demon had gone out, the dumb man spoke; and the multitudes marveled. But some of them said, "He casts out demons by Beelzebul, the ruler of demons." And others, to test Him, were demanding of Him a sign from Heaven. But He knew their thoughts, and said to them, "Any kingdom divided against itself is laid waste; and a house divided against itself falls. And if Satan also is divided against himself, how shall his kingdom stand? For you say that I cast out demons by Beelzebul. And if I by Beelzebul cast out demons, by whom do your sons cast them out? Consequently they shall be your judges. But if I cast out demons by the finger of God, then the kingdom of God has come upon you. When a strong

man, fully armed, guards his own homestead, his possessions are undisturbed; but when someone stronger than
he attacks him and overpowers him, he takes away from
him all his armor on which he had relied, and distributes
his plunder." (Lk 11:14-22)

Jesus and those of his day believed in the existence of
Satan. This "strong man's" homestead is the planet Earth,
and his possessions are the souls he has captured to take
with him to hell. He is fully armed with great power, but
Jesus has overpowered and plundered him. In Ephesians
1:22 the apostle Paul says, "And He put all things in
subjection under His feet, and gave Him as head over all
things to the church." In Jesus' name we have strength to
resist this strong man, and using the keys of the kingdom
that Jesus gave us we can set free Satan's captives.

It is crucial that every believer in Jesus understands that
he or she is involved in a conflict and knows how to engage
in spiritual warfare. Let me give you an example of how the
Lord taught this to me and my wife Kristina. When we were
on the island of Maui enjoying a much needed vacation, a
friend of ours whose name is Andy had met us on the island.
Andy was an executive in one of the most powerful media
conglomerates in the world and had been in the midst of
intensive spiritual warfare for over a year. This Fortune 500
corporation was run by people who were heavily involved
in New Age philosophy and practices. Several of the other
key executives had been officers in one of the largest and
most effective spiritual groups that had penetrated many of
the major corporations with its blend of Eastern mysticism
and high-tech motivational seminars. Andy had been

praying for over a year, binding the spirit of deception at work and praying for the salvation of people in the business. Unlike many Christians who have a tendency to retreat when the battle gets tough, Andy hung in there because he believed that God had placed him in his job for a purpose. So among the channeling, consciousness altering activities, and New Age doctrines, Andy walked in the power of the Holy Spirit in this veritable fiery furnace of the corporate arena because he had heard the voice of the Holy Spirit and he understood that many lives besides his own would be affected.

One evening in Maui all of us were watching the sun set on this lovely tropical isle. As we looked down at silvery waves crashing upon the rocks, Kristina spotted a dark crab-like creature climbing upon the rocks. It was difficult to see because it blended with the color of the rocks so perfectly. Kristina had noticed this creature just a few moments after Andy and I had begun talking about the spiritual warfare he was involved in. As she pointed us toward the rocks, we began to see many of these crab-like creatures camouflaged by the water and the color of the rocks. We could now pick out dozens of these creatures creeping upon the rocks. Andy realized that these sea creatures could only be seen by careful scrutiny and that they were invisible to the casual observer. The Holy Spirit spoke to Kristina and she told Andy that the camouflage of these sea creatures was like the many unseen spiritual creatures involved in the corporate conflict he was engaged in. Although Andy could not view them with his natural eyes, he was engaged in a serious conflict with them. Together, the three of us began to pray for the officers of his corporation as we watched the crab-like creatures hiding among the rocks. It was as if through this example in nature God had allowed us to peek into the invisible spiritual realm and see the demonic powers at work so that we could bind them in the name of Jesus Christ and call forth the influence of the Holy Spirit. When Andy returned to New York City, the atmosphere in his corporation completely changed. Andy told us that the New Age activity had fallen out of favor and had been driven underground.

The supernatural God of the universe speaks to his hildren through visual concepts in nature, situations, visions, and dreams. This is an authentic biblical pattern for heavenly communication. It should not be viewed as something strange or bizarre. In Acts 10:9-12 God spoke to Peter in a trance:

> And on the next day, as they were on their way, and approaching the city, Peter went up on the housetop about the sixth hour to pray. And he became hungry, and was desiring to eat; but while they were making preparations, he fell into a trance; and he beheld the sky opened up, and a certain object like a great sheet coming down, lowered by four corners to the ground, and there were in it all kinds of four-footed animals and crawling creatures of the earth and birds of the air.

God can and will use pictures and impressions to speak to us and call us to prayer. This is often the language of the Holy Spirit. As long as what is being pictured is within the parameters of the Scripture, there is nothing to fear. Listening to the voice of the Holy Spirit and letting God speak to you through visual impressions is not a call to never-

never land. It is a call from the Holy Spirit and produces effectiveness and maturity in the lives of believers who are committed to Christ and walking in obedience to the Word of God.

EVEN THE WIND AND THE SEA OBEY HIM

And there arose a fierce gale of wind, and the waves were breaking over the boat so much that the boat was already filling up. And He Himself was in the stern, asleep on the cushion; and they awoke Him, and said to Him, "Teacher, do you not care that we are perishing?" And being aroused, He rebuked the wind, and said to the sea, "Hush, be still." And the wind died down and it became perfectly calm. And He said to them, "Why are you so timid? How is it that you have no faith?" And they became very much afraid and said to one another, "Who then is this, that even the wind and the sea obey Him?" (Mk 4:37-41)

Our society is currently in the midst of a great spiritual storm and in fear many in our culture are turning to false gods for help. Yet Jesus Christ still says to the church today, "Why are you so fearful? How is it that you have no faith?" Faced with a powerful storm, Jesus exercised his supernatural authority over the natural elements and commanded the wind to silence and the storm to cease and both obeyed him. We need to understand that the authority that God gave Jesus Christ has been transferred to us. Matthew 7:29 says: "...For He was teaching them as one having authority, and not as their scribes." Jesus Christ was not just another spiritual teacher or guru. He taught as "one with authority."

So too in our culture there are many people communicating spiritual ideas and philosophies. But when we as Christians enter into the arena of human affairs we must like our Master be "one of authority." It is vital that we understand that Jesus Christ has given us his authority. "And He called the twelve together, and gave them power and authority over all the demons, and to heal diseases" (Lk 9:1).

Acts 4:33 reads, "And with great power the Apostles were giving witness to the resurrection of the Lord Jesus, and abundant grace was upon them all." God gives great power to believers who are united to him in praise and worship, and great grace will be upon anyone who moves in this power. This power is the supernatural favor of God at work in a hostile world. It transcends everyday realities and brings the miraculous kingdom of God within reach of any individual who has faith in Jesus and his Word.

Accompanying this great power is supernatural wisdom. Acts 6:10: "And yet they were unable to cope with the wisdom and the Spirit with which he [Stephen] was speaking." This supernatural wisdom is not relegated to first-century believers but is available to all Christians today. Above all we must come to realize that true biblical Christianity is not a comfortable armchair religion. It is a relationship with the living God which produces power to transform our world. This supernatural power and wisdom has extremely practical impact on every level of life.

SUPERNATURAL MEN AND WOMEN

The children of Israel encountered the supernatural God many times after they escaped from Egypt and the armies of

Pharaoh. They had seen Moses divide the Red Sea in the power of God, and they had been led miraculously by a pillar of cloud by day and a pillar of fire by night. In Exodus 19:16-19 Moses and the children of Israel encounter the supernatural God again.

> So it came about on the third day, when it was morning, that there were thunder and lightning flashes and a thick cloud upon the mountain and a very loud trumpet sound, so that all the people who were in the camp trembled. And Moses brought the people out of the camp to meet God, and they stood at the foot of the mountain. Now Mount Sinai was all in smoke because the Lord descended upon it in fire; and its smoke ascended like the smoke of a furnace, and the whole mountain quaked violently. When the sound of the trumpet grew louder and louder, Moses spoke and God answered him with thunder.

In the same way God wants to reveal himself in power to the people of our day who deny his existence, and to declare to his people and the nations that he is God and that he is alive forevermore.

Later on in Exodus we read about what happens to Moses, an ordinary man, as he comes in contact with God:

> And it came about when Moses was coming down from Mount Sinai (and the two tablets of the testimony were in Moses' hand as he was coming down from the mountain) that Moses did not know that the skin of his face shone because of his speaking with Him. So when Aaron and all the sons of Israel saw Moses, behold, the skin of his face

shone, and they were afraid to come near him. (Ex 34:29-30)

Moses was transformed by his supernatural encounter with God, as we should be. God's children need to be transformed in the presence of God so that they will have the power to transform their world. Each of us needs the glory of God shining through us so that we can reach out to the world. If we move out into our culture in mere human power, we will fail to transform our society because *we* have not been transformed. Nothing is more tragic than to see Christians confront the New Age with skimpy theological arguments and without the supernatural power of the Holy Spirit.

Because there have been abuses in the areas of miracles and healing some of us are hesitant to enter into a supernatural relationship with Jesus Christ and embrace the realm of the miraculous. But it is our responsibility before God to allow his presence and supernatural glory to come upon us. Acts 15:12 says:

And all the multitude kept silent, and they were listening to Barnabas and Paul as they were relating what signs and wonders God had done through them among the Gentiles.

Signs and wonders should accompany the preaching of the gospel. Anyone can talk about God—even the people in the New Age can do that. Christians need to communicate biblical truth with supernatural boldness and a verifiable demonstration of God's power. When you share Jesus Christ with someone, find out what the needs are or listen to the voice of the Holy Spirit and let God show you super-naturally what is going on in that person's life, and then pray for him or her with faith and boldness that God will miraculously intervene in their lives.

Biblical signs and wonders do not have to be spectacular miracles. Signs and wonders can include answered prayer concerning even the smallest things. Signs and wonders are simply God's actions in people's lives. God's healing may occur in spectacular ways, or in ordinary ways such as a restored marriage, a job, physical health, or freedom from depression. Signs and wonders can be seen in the life of any theological "camp." They occur in the lives of all who call on the name of the Lord. Real miracles are most often quiet and simple, and are easily overlooked unless you are seeing with the eyes of faith.

DELIVERANCE

Certain Eastern mystical practices can produce points of spiritual bondage in a person's life. If a person has opened the door to that unseen spiritual reality through various New Age or Eastern mystical practices, he may have inadver-tently opened the door to spiritual oppression—not neces-sarily possession but oppression.

As one who was personally involved in many of these activities for over a decade, I had developed psychic abilities by which I could receive all kinds of spiritual information at will. In other words, I was trained and practiced in being sensitive to the spiritual realm. When I became a Christian and received Jesus Christ into my life, these powers and forces didn't just disappear. As a new Christian I can remember being able to walk into a room and know immediately if anyone was involved in meditation, mysticism, or the occult. In fact, my acute spiritual sensitivity could be quite disorienting. I had a mind like a powerful radio receiver tuned to frequencies in the spiritual dimension, and I was unable to turn it off. Because I had spent so many years involved in mysticism I was still connected to it and invisible ties had to be severed. A fellow Christian who had experienced a similar thing came into my life. In the sanctuary of a church, Wayne laid hands on me and began to pray. As we worshiped God and prayed, Wayne took authority over these forces in my life in the name of Jesus and bound the work of the enemy. He pleaded the blood of Jesus Christ over me, and in that prayer the ties I had to this spiritual dimension were severed. This was a prayer of deliverance from oppression, the exercising of the authority of Jesus over my past involvement in mystical activities.

THE CONFRONTATION OF DARKNESS AND LIGHT

Magic, sorcery, astrology, and the occult were as rampant in the days of the Apostles as they are today. It is interesting to note how Paul dealt with these powers. What is recorded in the Book of Acts could be a working model for how Christians should preach the gospel and relate to the New

Age Movement of our day:

> And God was performing extraordinary miracles by the hands of Paul, so that handkerchiefs or aprons were even carried from his body to the sick, and the diseases left them and the evil spirits went out. But also some of the Jewish exorcists, who went from place to place, attempted to name over those who had the evil spirits the name of the Lord Jesus, saying, "I adjure you by Jesus whom Paul preaches." And seven sons of one Sceva, a Jewish chief priest, were doing this. And the evil spirit answered and said to them, "I recognize Jesus, and I know about Paul, but who are you?" And the man, in whom was the evil spirit, leaped on them and subdued all of them and over-powered them, so that they fled out of that house naked and wounded. And this became known to all, both Jews and Greeks, who lived in Ephesus; and fear fell upon them all and the name of the Lord Jesus was being magnified. Many also of those who had believed kept coming, confessing and disclosing their practices. And many of those who practiced magic brought their books together and began burning them in the sight of all; and they counted up the price of them and found it fifty thousand pieces of silver. So the word of the Lord was growing mightily and prevailing. (Acts 19:11-20)

Scripture says, "And God was performing extraordinary miracles by the hands of Paul." The biblical model for the effective Christian leader is that God performs extraordinary miracles through that individual. These miracles may manifest themselves in a myriad of ways, such as salvation, healing, deliverance, and wisdom, but the point is that the biblical model clearly indicates that God will perform miracles through Christians. Paul did not spend time arguing theology with those in the occult or mysticism. He demonstrated his supernatural authority with "extraordinary miracles."

This power is in distinct contrast to many of the Christians in our day who attempt to reach people involved in the supernatural through arguing, debating theology, and attempting to prove to these people that they are wrong by presenting to them a series of Bible verses.

There is nothing inherently wrong with quoting Scripture, for "the word of God is living and active and sharper than any two-edged sword, piercing as far as the division of soul and spirit, of both joints and marrow, and able to judge the thoughts and intentions of the heart" (Heb 4:12). There is tremendous power in sharing the Word of God. But the biblical model does not stop there. God is showing us a precise plan in his Word for winning people who are involved in the New Age and other occult activities, and that is to allow him to work miracles through us so that people will be converted to Jesus Christ.

A SPIRIT OF DIVINATION

We have seen how major corporations are being infiltrated by the New Age Movement, astrologers, and psychics. However, if we go back to New Testament times we see that the merger of business and the occult has been around for centuries. In Acts 16:16-19 we read an account of Paul's encounter with a slave girl who had a spirit of divination and who was involved with local merchants in the business of fortune-telling:

> And it happened that as we were going to the place of prayer, a certain slave girl having a spirit of divination met us, who was bringing her masters much profit by fortune-telling. Following after Paul and us, she kept crying out, saying, "These men are bondservants of the Most High God, who are proclaiming to you the way of salvation." And she continued doing this for many days. But Paul was greatly annoyed, and turned and said to the spirit, "I command you in the name of Jesus Christ to come out of her!" And it came out that very moment. But when her master saw that their hope of profit was gone, they seized Paul and Silas and dragged them into the market place before the authorities.

As in other places in the Bible, Paul has come into contact with direct spiritual opposition. It is interesting to note that the spirit of divination recognized who Paul and Silas were and proceeded to harass them. Paul did not allow this occult activist to attack him constantly. Eventually, Paul exercised his authority in Jesus Christ and said to the spirit, "I command you in the name of Jesus Christ to come out of her!" Paul recognized that he was not fighting a flesh and blood person but a spirit from hell. We must also recognize that we are not always fighting flesh and blood but evil spirits and demons.

This exercise of supernatural authority was costly for Paul

and Silas for it disrupted the profit that the local business-men were making. When we exercise our spiritual authority it may also cost us something because the powers of hell do not like to be challenged. This does not mean that we have anything to fear; God caused Paul and Silas to triumph even in jail when he sent a great earthquake to release them. But living in the flow of supernatural power can be disruptive to our everyday lives.

When dealing with spirits of divination or people with psychic powers, we should have the same confidence that Paul had. This does not mean that we are just to walk up to people involved in the occult and cast spirits out of them. Paul was responding to specific direction of the Holy Spirit. However, in the course of my business activities I regularly encounter men and women who are involved in occult spiritual activity. Sometimes I can tell the presence of an evil spirit or if someone is involved in spiritual activity, sexual perversion, or extreme deception. I am not always sure what kind of spirit I am dealing with, but I silently bind the powers of darkness over that person and the room in the name of Jesus Christ. In this way, I am stopping great harm that could be done and allowing the kingdom of God to rule. Sometimes it is necessary to bind the forces or powers of darkness over a home or a specific geographic location. Many times when I am walking in Hollywood I am praying silently and not only binding the powers of darkness but calling upon the Holy Spirit to be poured out.

The Church On The Way in California recently had hundreds of men of the church go to key geographic locations overlooking the city of Los Angeles to pray for the city and claim it for Jesus Christ. This is not superstition but taking the mandate of Christ to "bind the strong man" and exercise spiritual dominion. I recently walked around the borders of my home up in the Hollywood Hills and prayed for supernatural protection around my house and my neighbors' houses and bound the powers of darkness against attack. I am also aware of the prevalence of people meditating, dealing drugs, and practicing witchcraft in my community, so I have bound the darkness over my community and called down the saving power of God. As God's men and women it is our responsibility to do this. If we don't then we cannot complain if all hell breaks loose. Let us pray that "all heaven will break loose." Instead of crime and occult forces there will be salvation, healing, and revival. Like modern Elijahs we can call down the fire of God on our homes and communities by praying a prayer such as this: "Father, in the name of Jesus Christ I bind the powers of darkness over my home, community, and neighborhood. I call down your Holy Spirit to be poured out and to save, heal, and deliver people. I thank you for doing this and believe that the kingdom of God is pushing out the darkness!"

SERVANTHOOD, NOT GODHOOD

The New Age teaches that we are gods and the great cosmic goal is to achieve godhood by working out your *karma*. In Christianity, Jesus himself becomes a servant. In fact, Jesus Christ models for us with his life what true spirituality is really all about. Philippians 2:4-11 says:

> Do not merely look out for your own personal interests, but also for the interests of others. Have this attitude in yourselves which was also in Christ Jesus, who, although He existed in the form of God, did not regard equality with God a thing to be grasped, but emptied Himself, taking the form of a bond-servant, and being made in the likeness of men. And being found in appearance as a man, He humbled Himself by becoming obedient to the point of death, even death on a cross. Therefore also God highly exalted Him, and bestowed on Him the name which is above every name, that at the name of Jesus every knee should bow, of those who are in heaven, and on earth, and under the earth, and that every tongue should confess that Jesus Christ is Lord, to the glory of God the Father.

Jesus Christ is not like all the gurus and spiritual teachers of our day who love to own luxury mansions and be exalted in positions of influence. The Bible states that Jesus Christ "existed in the form of God, did not regard equality with God a thing to be grasped" (Phil 2:6). The apostle Paul urges us to have "this attitude in yourselves which was also in Christ Jesus" (Phil 2:5). In Jesus Christ we see the biblical model for servanthood and humility—divine love is expressed in self-sacrifice.

Paul writes, "Do not merely look out for your own personal interests, but also for the interests of others" (Phil 2:4), and, "Do nothing from selfishness or empty conceit, but with humility of mind let each of you regard one another as more important than himself" (Phil 2:3). This flies in the face of everything our culture teaches us and what much of the church practices. It defies the major tenets of the New Age Movement.

Paul also says, "Owe nothing to anyone except to love one another; for he who loves his neighbor has fulfilled the law" (Rom 13:8). Ultimately it is the practice of this principle which wins people to Jesus Christ. Things like spiritual gifts and miracles are absolutely useless without love behind them. What distinguishes Christianity from the New Age and other religions is the fact that a relationship with Jesus Christ produces love for others.

The spirituality that Jesus Christ taught was not an esoteric teaching. It manifested itself in such practical things as feeding the hungry, clothing the poor, and bringing healing to all who need it. Spiritual enlightenment is promised not to those who sit in a lotus position and contemplate their navels, or to those who leave their bodies in astral projection, or even to those who never act upon the Bible but only study it in a manner removed from practical application. Spiritual understanding is promised to those who put their love into action and minister to the poor, hungry, downtrodden, oppressed, and needy. The prophet Isaiah says,

Then your light will break out like the dawn,
And your recovery will speedily spring forth;
And your righteousness will go before you;
The glory of the Lord will be your rear guard.
Then you will call, and the Lord will answer;

You will cry, and He will say, "Here I am."
If you remove the yoke from your midst, the pointing of the finger, and speaking wickedness,
And if you give yourself to the hungry, and satisfy the desire of the afflicted. (Is 58:8-10)

SIX

Reclaiming Our World for Christ

ACCORDING TO A RECENT SURVEY by George Gallup, Jr., president of the Gallup Poll of opinion leaders, only twenty-nine percent of American people feel that organized religion is giving adequate answers to "moral problems and the needs of the individual." In addition, twenty-five percent feel that organized religion isn't giving adequate solutions to the problems of family life and only thirty-five percent believe that man's spiritual needs are being fulfilled by organized religion.[1]

Obviously, these opinion leaders did not feel that organized religion offered meaningful answers to the larger body of our population. Any casual observer of American life would have to concur with these observations. For even though earlier Gallup Poll figures revealed that fifty million people in the United States claimed to be "born again," many Christians have a very spurious commitment to their faith. For example, according to a Gallup Poll survey for *Christianity Today* done in 1978, ninety-four percent of

Americans believed in God or a "universal spirit." But only sixty-nine percent believed that "God or this spirit observes their actions and rewards or punishes them for their actions."[2] These statistics reveal that most Americans' faith in God is rather vague and is somewhat superficial and shallow. In other words, we have millions who say they believe in Jesus Christ but very few who are disciples of Jesus Christ.

In 1957, sixty-nine percent of the population felt that "religion was increasing its influence." However, in 1981, only thirty-eight percent of the population felt this way, and forty-six percent felt that religion was actually losing its influence.[3] Statistics on abortion, divorce, AIDS, suicide, alcoholism, drug addiction, violent crime, and white-collar crime seem to support this. For on every hand we see a continual escalation of sociological problems that have distinct spiritual roots.

If Jesus Christ commanded the church to "go into all the world and preach the gospel," then we have failed to do this in our own culture. The United States is a post-Christian nation where the vast majority of people do not have a biblical faith in God. In addition, a new generation is growing up which has been turned off to Christianity and which is spiritually hungry. In the book *Hare Krishna and the Counterculture,* J. Stillson Judah, a professor of the History of Religions and Director of the Graduate Theological Union Common Library in Berkley, California, did a study of why young people left Christianity for the Hare Krishna Movement. The Hare Krishna Movement is a religious movement based on ancient Hinduism and promoted in the West by the Indian guru A.C. Bhaktivedanta Swami Prabhupada. It teaches that you can reach Krishna consciousness or cosmic consciousness, a means of entering Paradise, by chanting the names of the mythological Hindu god Krishna. According to Judah's survey, seventy percent of the Krishna devotees' parents are members of one of the established churches and 64.5 percent had attended their parents' church regularly before joining the Hindu sect. Furthermore, seventy-six percent abandoned their former faith because of "its incapacity to develop an experience of God"; 67.5 percent left due to "its incapacity to give a larger meaning of life," and 62.5 percent could not "develop a close meaningful fellowship."[4]

The statistics regarding why young people left the Christian church for the Hare Krishna Movement provide a microcosm for why the entire New Age Movement is spreading and why the Christian church has failed to penetrate society.

RECLAIMING THE GOVERNMENT AND CORPORATE AMERICA

The Bible gives specific guidelines concerning reaching those in positions of leadership and in ordinary life who are involved in occult philosophies. Since the beginning of time governments and business enterprises have been consulting astrologers, psychics, seers, mediums, and magicians. In the Book of Daniel we read the story of one of God's servants who became a ruler and government and business consultant to King Nebuchadnezzar. Here is a model of how God wants us to deal with the New Age Movement as it relates to both corporate America and government.

In the beginning of the Book of Daniel we see that King Nebuchadnezzar was doing some executive recruiting and looking for men who could advise him in economic, spiritual, and political matters. Daniel 1:4 says that Nebuchadnezzar was looking for "youths in whom was no defect, who were good looking, showing intelligence in every branch of wisdom, endowed with understanding, and discerning knowledge, and who had ability for serving in the king's court; and he ordered him to teach them the language of the Chaldeans." The King was looking for men of exceptional character and development. God was ushering his own men into the King's court so that he could accomplish his purposes. What appeared to be mere political activity and executive recruitment was orchestrated by God to accomplish his purpose. Furthermore, God gave Daniel supernatural or divine favor that transcended his natural abilities: "Now God granted Daniel favor and compassion in the sight of the commander and officials" (Dn 1:9).

In addition, God gave Daniel and his associates supernatural wisdom and intelligence. In effect, the Spirit of God amplified their natural intelligence as well as giving them direct contact with his omniscience when it was necessary: "And as for these four youths, God gave them knowledge and intelligence in every branch of literature and wisdom; Daniel even understood all kinds of visions and dreams" (Dn 1:17).

Here we see men of God in government and what could be viewed as a corporate structure. These men of God faced the same intense competitiveness, networking, power plays, and politics as any of their modern counterparts in the corporate jungle. Furthermore, this bureaucracy was heavily immersed in occult activity. Notice Daniel and his associates allowed the Spirit of God to give them supernatural wisdom and insight into the challenges facing their government.

Daniel and his associates earned the respect of their employer and the other staff by demonstrating wisdom over a period of time. Their superior expertise and counsel placed them in a position of stature and prominence. When the King faced the problem of interpreting his dream, he called "the magicians, the conjurers, the sorcerers and the Chaldeans" for help. They failed. So when Daniel gave the King the correct interpretation of the dream, God was glorified. Daniel did not spend his time arguing theology with the magicians, conjurers, and sorcerers. He did not point the finger at them and tell them they were deceived and following the Devil. Nor did he begin quoting scriptures at them or give them his testimony. Daniel allowed God's supernatural power to fight the battle and demonstrated the reality of his faith with revelational knowledge and power.

A corporate crisis was occurring in the kingdom and the King threatened to kill all of his advisors unless they correctly interpreted the dream. None of those involved in the occult or mysticism had the power to interpret Nebuchadnezzar's dream. However, when Daniel asked God for the answer, God gave Daniel supernatural business advice:

Then the mystery was revealed to Daniel in a night vision. Then Daniel blessed the God of heaven; Daniel answered and said, "Let the name of God be blessed forever and ever, For wisdom and power belong to Him. And it is He who changes the times and the epochs: He removes kings and establishes kings; He gives wisdom to wise men, And knowledge to men of understanding. It is He who reveals the profound and hidden things; He knows what is in the darkness, And the light dwells with Him. To Thee, O God of my fathers, I give thanks and praise, For Thou hast given me wisdom and power; Even now Thou hast made known to me what we requested of Thee, For Thou hast made known to us the king's matter." (Dn 2:19-23)

Daniel did not make the mistake of merely relying on his natural intelligence and abilities as many contemporary Christian business men and leaders do. Nor did he throw away his natural education, intelligence, or training. Daniel sought God for answers first; in this business crisis where he and many others could have lost their very lives, he went to God for help. King Nebuchadnezzar was witnessed to in a powerful way and acknowledged the reality of God. In Daniel 2:46-49 we see that Nebuchadnezzar literally "fell on his face" before Daniel and promoted him:

Then King Nebuchadnezzar fell on his face and did homage to Daniel, and gave orders to present to him an offering and fragrant incense. The king answered Daniel and said, "Surely your God is a God of gods and a Lord of kings and a revealer of mysteries, since you have been able to reveal this mystery." Then the king promoted Daniel and gave him many great gifts, and he made him ruler over the whole province of Babylon and chief prefect over all the wise men of Babylon. And Daniel made request of the king, and he appointed Shadrach, Meshach and Abed-nego over the province of Babylon, while Daniel was at the king's court.

Daniel did not allow himself to speak glibly or idly about his God. He chose his words wisely. The occult and Eastern mysticism were all around him, but Daniel did not spend his time in useless arguments with the magicians and sorcerers, telling them they were deceived and that they needed to repent. Daniel moved in God's timing and allowed the Holy Spirit to use him as a vehicle. He walked in purity, humility, and integrity before the Lord and so God was able to use him. The whole corporate and bureaucratic world of Babylon was shaken to the core. God wants to inspire men and women in business today and give supernatural solutions to contemporary problems. The same Spirit which moved upon Daniel is available today.

APPLYING THE BIBLICAL PATTERN TO RECLAIM OTHER PROFESSIONS

The Holy Spirit is the source of all wisdom, and the wisdom of God is endlessly creative and alive. It is not stale, dull, and boring. The wisdom of God which is available to man through the Holy Spirit and through the Word of God is the highest source of intelligence available. Behind the spoken Word of God which framed the universe, hung the stars, sent the sun and moon spinning into space, and created all that is, was the intelligence and wisdom of God. And in line with the generous character of God, he makes this infinite wisdom available to his children.

We need to open ourselves to his eternal wisdom and revelation in the spirit of Daniel, Joseph, and Paul. We live in the hour when God is sending his supernatural knowledge to men and women of all walks of life. The creative Spirit of God has answers for scientists regarding everything from the mysteries of creation to new energy sources. God can show politicians how to transcend party politics and become true statesmen who can bring healing and unity to our divided nation. The Lord is able to give bankers unique understanding of debt ratios and answers regarding the national debt and its effect on interlocking economies. Teachers can be equipped to educate more effectively. Biologists and medical doctors can gain insight from God regarding cures for diseases like AIDS and cancer. Ministers can receive visions for effective programs to serve the poor, homeless, hungry, and destitute. And psychologists can exercise unique understanding regarding mental health problems.

On every hand, wisdom from an unseen dimension—the domain of the personal living God of the universe—can be transmitted to our world. The time has come for God's people to allow him to amplify their human intelligence through the power of the Holy Spirit and give them supernatural wisdom. But the goal of his power in us is *love*. Whatever we receive from God is given out of his love for us and his desire to see us love others. Ambition, power, control, or success should not rule children of God. Only in love can we be channels of healing in our world.

COMMUNICATING LOVE

It is important for Christians to know how to communicate the truth and power of God to the world. First, we must understand that the foundation of all we say and do should be love. The apostle Paul says in 1 Corinthians 13:1 "If I speak with the tongues of men and of angels, but do not have love, I have become a noisy gong or a clanging cymbal." It is sad to say, but we have a lot of clanging cymbals and noisy gongs for Jesus out there and nowhere is this more true than in our efforts to evangelize the New Age. A spirit of self-righteousness often infects our communication with people in the New Age Movement. The idea that "I'm right and you're wrong" can be transmitted without even saying a word.

Jesus did not call us to be self-righteous and spiritually superior. Our salvation rests totally on the grace of God, so what do we have to be proud of anyway? Yet, when it comes to things like sharing the life of Jesus Christ with people involved in mysticism and the New Age, Christians can be very ugly; it all boils down to a lack of love and true commitment to other people. God did not call us to win arguments but to win souls, and in order for us to be effective at bringing others to Christ we must move in the power of the Holy Spirit with humility and wisdom.

First of all, we must understand that many people are in the New Age Movement because they have never seen true biblical Christianity lived out before them. We need to be sensitive to the needs of people, listen to them, and accept them as they are. Many of these people simply have never heard the gospel or known people whose lives have been transformed by it. Many have never experienced the love of God through another person, or seen God's character expressed in their neighbor's words and deeds. The media doesn't tell them the truth about God, their families haven't known him, and their schools have left him out of the curriculum. When you encounter someone in the New Age, never underestimate your value as a messenger of God's love and truth.

Here are some principles or suggested guidelines that you can apply when communicating to people involved in the New Age, the occult, or false religions:

1. Pray for the other person or group regularly before you speak. Intercede for them and actually bind the work of the enemy in their lives. This is not to imply that all those involved in the New Age are demon-possessed or actively following powers of darkness. Most people involved in the New Age Movement, mysticism, and the occult are completely unaware of a spiritual battle that is going on. Effective prayer involves binding the forces of darkness should they be operating in a given situation. (See Ephesians 6:12 and 18-19.)

2. Love the people you are relating to and communicating with. Ministry comes out of relationship, and if you haven't taken the time to develop a friendship you probably shouldn't talk about Jesus Christ. Real love involves true caring and commitment to another person. (See 1 John 4:7-11.)

3. Do not have a hidden agenda or manipulate someone when you are relating to them. No one likes to be used or conned or tricked into hearing about Christ. People can see right through you if your only purpose in being nice to them is to tell them about Jesus. This isn't real love, it is manipulation—if you are honest with yourself you are not really loving the other person but simply trying to put a notch on your belt by winning someone to Christ. Winning people to Christ is not a numbers game. It involves a quality commitment to other people as people and not simply as "objects" to be saved. If you really love someone you won't have to say much. People can tell the difference between real love and an ulterior motive. (See 1 Corinthians 13:8.)

4. *Don't lay trips on people.* Walking up to someone and telling them they are going to burn in hell if they don't receive Jesus, or shouting at them to repent, or simply repeating that Jesus is the only way to God is not ministering to people. What you have to say may be true but you have communicated it in such a destructive manner that you will have done more harm than good. In addition, you will have reinforced their worst preconceptions about Christianity and will have placed a barrier between them and Jesus Christ. (See 1 Corinthians 13:4.)

5. *Give intelligent answers.* People have honest questions about God and the Bible. In sensitivity take the time to give intelligent explanations for what you believe. (see 2 Timothy 2:15.)

6. *Speak wisely and under the anointing of the Holy Spirit.* When talking about Jesus Christ you should be led and guided by the Holy Spirit. (See Proverbs 15:2.)

If you want to reach people for Jesus Christ, you can start by praying for God to direct you to the people he wants to reach. Then you can befriend these people and really get to

know them and enjoy them. Ministry comes out of relationship, and you can develop relationships by inviting people
home for dinner or taking them out to lunch. Don't do this in
a mechanical and manipulative manner, with an ulterior
motive, or out of a sense of guilt. Do this out of a desire to
really get to know someone and be involved in his life. Then
if the Holy Spirit prompts you and a door is open, feel free to
share about your life with God. Don't try to convert them.
Simply share what God has done in your life and don't
"bang them over the head with the Bible." If they respect
you as a person, they will listen to what you have to say.

TRANSLATE THE BIBLE TO EVERYDAY LIFE

The Bible speaks to political issues, science, law, sexuality,
marriage, business, sociology, history, art, literature, and a
wide spectrum of life. I cannot tell you how many churches I
have visited where the minister seemed to be speaking from
the stratosphere with theological phrases and words like
redemption, sanctification, eschatology, millennialism, regen-
eration, and so on. Even well-meaning sermons seem to float
like clouds above the heads of the people. Many times I have
said to myself, "What does all this mean to my life in the real
world? How do the words of Jesus Christ and the Bible
apply to the nitty-gritty details of my life?" Let us ask
ourselves how the Bible speaks to these needs:
—My marriage is breaking up.
—My boss hates me.
—My career is going nowhere.
—I am depressed.

—Nightmares torment me.

—I have unpaid bills.

—My sexual desire is strong, and I'm single (or divorced).

—I want to get ahead at work.

—My husband has a drinking problem and is not a Christian.

—I have homosexual desires.

—I am a Christian and I have a problem with pornography.

—I am addicted to drugs.

—I am a victim of child abuse.

—I am an adult child of an alcoholic and I can't break free from the psychological bondage.

—I feel that I have so much potential in life, but I can't seem to unlock it.

—I want to get over my fears and phobias.

—I'm lonely and all my Christian friends just quote scriptures at me.

—I feel like a failure.

Many sermons dance around these issues or simply slap a few scriptures on them and urge people to pray. People who have real problems need to know how to apply the power of Jesus to them.

The goal is not to imitate the New Age Movement or adapt Scripture to its false view of reality. The goal is to communicate biblical truths meaningfully and understandably to a new generation. How do we bring the supernatural power of God and the miraculous dimension of Christianity into our world? The following is a list of key areas for us to consider:

—the authority of Scripture as it applies to all of life;

—how the power of the Holy Spirit and the Spirit-filled life transforms individuals, families, and society;

—the reality of spiritual warfare and the power of prayer;

—the importance of worship;

—the miraculous dimension of Christianity;

—the importance of unity and love;

—what Scripture teaches about practical issues: money, jobs, marriage, family, relationships, sex, mental and emotional well-being, and health and divine healing;

—what Scripture teaches about social issues: world peace, ecology, the poor and homeless, the mentally ill, civil rights, women's issues, world hunger, war, and poverty.

Often contemporary preaching contains theology removed from real life, or renounces what is wrong in the world without clear guidance on what is right. In response to the call to holiness, some Christians don't drink, dance, smoke, swear, or go to movies. But what do Christians *do*? Is holiness based on what you *don't* do? Christianity that is defined by negatives misses the point of what God is trying to *do*: empower a chosen generation to create alternate cultures based on the Word of God. Christianity leads to a life marked by joy, celebration, and creativity. We serve the Creator of the universe who is the maker of all good things.

CREATE A NEW WORLD VISION

What I have seen in much of the contemporary Christian culture is rather shallow. Its capacity to be an effective agent of change in our society often does not hold much promise.

Nowhere is this more evident than in the area of global crisis where Christians throw off their responsibility for stewardship and replace it with pronouncements of Christ's soon return. Yes, Jesus Christ is coming, but we are not to wait passively for him. We are to be committed to our fellowman and society, and that means rolling up our sleeves and working for positive change. The New Age Movement is busy providing leadership and creating alternatives for our culture—alternatives and leadership that the Christian culture should be providing.

All across the world, major conferences and symposiums are being held that will shape the future of our planet and many are devoid of Christian leaders. Such conferences will deal with topics like tangible solutions for our common future, networking global consciousness, global issues which require immediate attention, and a whole spiritual-political agenda that will coordinate the human potential movement, the scientific community, political groups, diplomats, environmental experts, and activists.

In the scientific and medical fields, global New Age conferences are being organized that will transform the worlds of medical technology, hospitals, psychiatry, nutrition, and education. Once again, we see Christians absent from the debate.

Clearly, a new world vision is being created and one must wonder why Christians have not made their voices heard. Is it because of a conspiracy to lock them out? I believe the real reason is that many biblical Christians have removed themselves from the battle through a theology of "retreatism."

Demos Shakarian, the founder of the Full Gospel Business Men's Fellowship International, writes:

. . . Imagine what would happen if every Christian business person turned just half of his or her creative thinking time over to the problems now facing our world. . . . For example, if just a million Christian business men began thinking as hard about the problem of feeding the poor as they think about [making] a living, we'd have the problem licked in no time! What if a million more men and women were challenged to think about reaching the unreached tribes, and a million others were asked to think about housing the homeless? Still another million could be asked to give their best thinking to caring for the sick or ending AIDS. God could use that concentrated thought power to bring health and healing to the world. Instead we are asked to work on a church board or a committee. We read minutes and attend meetings. We may pound nails on a Saturday morning or witness door-to-door. We take directions from the clergy and do the jobs they assign us. But what would happen if they said to us, "Here's a *real* problem. Think about solving it and come back when you have the answer." Right now I'm telling God, "I want to go back out into the world. I want to think about your dreams for the people of this planet and what I can do to help those dreams come true." God is doing a new thing. Now is the time to get moving. Now is the time to conquer. Now is the time to catch the new wave of God's Spirit.[5]

TAKING OUR WORLD FOR CHRIST

I believe in planning, I believe in strategy, I believe in organizations and job descriptions and standards of performance. I believe in organizational charts . . . they have their place. But, nothing is of any value that man designs unless the Spirit of God is upon it and the only way we can expect to see our cities reached for Christ is that we who believe in Christ truly live supernatural lives. . . . We are not called to mediocrity; the moment we receive Christ, the incredible, incomparable Savior in whom dwells all the fullness of the Godhead bodily, the visible expression of the invisible God, the One to whom God has given all authority in heaven and earth literally comes to live within you and me. When we receive Christ, our bodies become temples of the living God—Father, Son, and Holy Ghost. We are no longer ordinary people at that precise moment. We become men and women of destiny. There's royal blood in our veins, we are children of God, heirs of God, joint heirs with Christ.[6]

These words were spoken by Dr. Bill Bright, President and founder of Campus Crusade for Christ, in 1987 at the Church on the Way in Van Nuys, California, at a Pastors' Conference. Dr. Bright's ministry has won millions of souls to Jesus Christ. I had the privilege of working with Campus Crusade for Christ while also serving as Director of the Concert Ministries of the Lamb's Club in New York City during the I FOUND IT Campaign. The Lamb's Club was a ministry of the Manhattan Church of The Nazarene under the direction of Reverend Paul Moore. Reverend Moore, who is now head of Campus Crusade for Christ's Inner City Ministries, used bold and daring evangelistic approaches to reach people with the message of God's love. While at the Lamb's Club, he created and I hosted a Christian nightclub in the Broadway Theatre District of New York City located near Times Square, a Christian professional theater, telethons, concerts, an outreach to the poor, and several other ministries to touch New York City for Jesus Christ.

Paul Moore and Bill Bright are men with creative approaches to reaching people for Jesus Christ. The I FOUND IT campaign was an example of a highly imaginative and unique concept in evangelism which helped take the message of God's love beyond the four walls of the church. The current *Jesus* film used by Campus Crusade has brought the message of the gospel to over 320 million people. Recently, at the Church on the Way, hundreds of home groups used the film as a tool to expose the people of Los Angeles to biblical truth.

These are examples of bold new approaches to reaching people with the gospel of Jesus Christ in our generation. At this same Pastors' Conference, Dr. Bright issued a challenge: "We are called to be world changers, we are called to be salt and light. Can you imagine our little finite beings linked up with the life of the infinite Creator God and remaining the same? We are called to live supernaturally for the glory of God." Then Dr. Bright charged believers:

—We must learn how to think supernaturally.

—Pray supernaturally.

—Plan supernaturally.

—Appropiate the supernatural power of God.
—Believe God for supernatural results.

SUPERNATURAL CREATIVITY AND THE MEDIA

Let's take a look at a medium in our culture that could use supernatural influence. If the motion picture industry has been around for almost a century and has become the most powerful means of communication the world has ever known, why have Christians had little or no influence on mainstream filmmaking? Where are the film programs in Christian schools, seminaries, and colleges who advertise that they are equipping the new generation for service, to reach our culture for Christ?

Lloyd Billingsley, a screenwriter who lives in California and who is a Christian, said in an interview with *Los Angeles Times*, "False pietism pronounces the whole area of popular culture off-limits for Christians. Christians won't sponsor a film unless the Gospel gets in. They want every film to evangelize or to be a Bible lesson—something film does very poorly."[7]

A new generation of Christian filmmakers, writers, producers, actors, and executives must arise who will not be content with making films in the church basement, who want to find ways to communicate their worldview in the mass culture entertainment format like 1981 Academy Award winner "Chariots of Fire."

Already the signs of this new trend are emerging. The First Presbyterian Church of Hollywood has created an Inter-

Mission Program which ministers to the entertainment community through dinners and discussion groups in a loving and creatively nurturing atmosphere. In a recent gathering the stars and producers of the CBS comedy "Designing Women," NBC's "The Today Show," and CBS's "The Equalizer" gathered to discuss "Today's Challenge: Walking as a Committed Christian in the Entertainment Industry." Also, Dr. Larry Poland, founder of Master Media and formerly with Campus Crusade for Christ, is actively ministering to key film and television executives through one-to-one ministry and intimate gatherings. Dr. Ted Baehr, who years ago was involved in some Cannon Films, is developing new ways to shape our culture with a biblical worldview through his "People and the Book" series and "Movie Guide."

LEARN HOW TO FIGHT FOR WHAT IS RIGHT

It has been said that the only thing necessary for evil to triumph is for good men to do nothing. This is exactly what is happening in our day as moral and righteous men and Christians sit back and passively watch our nation be taken over by those who have an agenda which is openly hostile to our Judeo-Christian beliefs and the holy commandments of God.

Do you realize the storm of protest that would occur if television programs were anti-gay, anti-feminist, or anti-minority? Yet Christians remain completely passive in the face of a constant and unrelenting assault on their religious culture. Why are the Christians in America not being taught from every pulpit, seminary, and Christian school to stand up for what is right?

In 1985 Rob Epstein and Richard Schmiechen won Oscars for the *Life and Times of Harvey Milk,* an account of the life and death of a gay activist. In a *Los Angeles Times* article dated June 24, 1988, writer Judith Michaelson writes:

> On three separate occasions documentary filmmakers Rob Epstein and Richard Schmiechen pitched their idea and a sample reel for a film on slain San Francisco Supervisor Harvey Milk to the Corporation of Public Broadcasting. And three times CPB, the non-profit organization that distributes federal funds for public television, turned them down. . . . After their third rejection from CPB—the last time because, they were told, they couldn't apply more than twice on the same project—they went back to the grueling task of outside fund-raising. . . . *The Life and Times of Harvey Milk* aired on PBS in November 1985, following a theatrical release. It had already won the 1984 Oscar for best documentary feature and would garner three Emmys for public television.[8]

These filmmakers had tenacity and perseverance and would not take no for an answer, and they were successful in communicating their message to millions of people. I wonder if this had been a group of Christian filmmakers, would they have thought, after confronting several obstacles, that God was closing the door? Would they give up because the task was fraught with difficulties?

It seems in certain quarters of the Christian culture that tenacity, guts, stick-to-itiveness, and perseverance are too aggressive, not properly meek and mild. All the while, secular activists go after their goals, produce results, and institute change. Whose worldview in relationship to politics and social responsibility is more biblical? The Christian who lives and teaches apathy in the name of spirituality or the New Age activist who preaches hard work, vision, and dedication?

TELEVISION

Shirley MacLaine's television movie *Out on a Limb* was a powerful sermon for the New Age Movement. In fact, B. Dalton Bookseller reported a ninety percent jump in sales of occult and astrology books immediately following the movie broadcasting. Television networks not only tend to attack or belittle Christianity, but also often actively promote Eastern mystical and New Age ideas. For behind the scenes in Hollywood, a majority of the writers, stars, producers, and directors are not only not Christians but many of them practice some form of Eastern religion.

I have been at many Hollywood parties where psychics give readings, astrologers interpret zodiac charts, and people play with crystals or talk about their channeling experiences. I remember having to locate a casting director for one of the films I was producing, and I had to call an ashram on the East Coast. As I waited for the casting director to come to the phone I could hear people chanting OM in the background. I have friends who have been in cars with major actors who have released the steering wheel and allowed a channeled entity to do the driving. I was on a movie set where one of the stars felt that he had come into contact with the spirit of the Marquis De Sade.

These are the people who are the creative force behind Hollywood. The majority of them have written off Christianity altogether as a "bad experience."

Christians must begin to produce television programs that communicate a biblical worldview for mass audiences. Pat Robertson's Christian Broadcasting Network seems to be the lone pioneer in producing mainstream programming from a Christian worldview. The other Christian networks and television ministries must begin to create development departments and begin to fund films, docu-dramas, and hard news programs. The day of Christian programming consisting of one man behind a pulpit is becoming anachronistic. Statistics show that the secular audience (the ones who are supposed to be reached) just aren't tuning in.

THE ARTS

The time has come for Christian artists in painting, sculpture, dance, theater, literature, and other forms of creative expression to come to the forefront. Christian artists must aggressively begin to exhibit in galleries and force the artistic establishment to take notice. The art galleries of New York, Chicago, Los Angeles, and other major cities should contain the work of Christian artists and if they are not allowed in, then they should start their own galleries. Christian choreographers must produce dance productions that perform around the world. The time for excuses has ended. A new day is here and we must move boldly into it.

SPOKESPEOPLE AND LEADERS

There are numerous outstanding leaders in the Christian culture, men such as Billy Graham, Pat Robertson, Dr. James Kennedy, Dr. James Dobson, Bill Bright, and Reverend Jack Hayford. However, a new generation of leadership must emerge that in time can assume their place.

We have a professional clergy of ministers who have taken the public role of leadership. But where are the lay people? The film producers, actors, corporate executives, social activists, politicians who will assume a public identity for Christ? Thankfully there have been some, but we need many more. Where are the Christian Jane Fondas who are smart, aggressive, and articulate spokespeople for their cause? Where are the CEOs of major corporations who will publicly be identified with Christ? In the world of athletics there seem to be many who are not afraid to stand for Christ, and this boldness needs to be expanded to other areas as well.

BUSINESS AND CORPORATE AMERICA

A new generation of young business men and women needs to be reached. This new generation needs to know how biblical principles apply to business, finance, investments, banking, sales, merchandising, and trade.

As I have said, organizations like Werner Erhard's est and Transformational Technologies and the many other New Age or humanistic groups have made considerable advances in the corporate arena. Hundreds of millions of dollars are spent by major corporations annually to solicit help from New Age-oriented organizations in the fields of motivation, sales training, and productivity. It is refreshing to see some Christian groups rise to the needs of the corporate world as well. Organizations like the Full Gospel Business Men's Fellowship International have had a powerful worldwide impact on individual businessmen and have been used by the Holy Spirit to bring hundreds of thousands to Christ. Organizations like the Christian Business Men's Committee have also provided a platform to communicate the reality of the Bible to businessmen. However, many more Christians need to join this wave of evangelism and aggressively take back the ground gained by the New Age.

POLITICS

As New Age activists merge with mainline political parties, they are going to gain more political clout. Already a New Age "think tank" in California has been successful in getting the state of California to fund a massive educational program on self-esteem which includes many New Age practices. We are going to see more of this in the future and we must be prepared for it.

In the area of politics Christians have been extremely successful and have begun making a difference at the national and local levels. Organizations like Beverly LaHaye's Concerned Women of America have successfully mobilized Christian women across the country to pray for and change our society. Women are an extremely powerful resource for changing this society and can often be far more effective than men because they are more persistent. This is why the radical feminist movement has been so powerful.

However, despite the excellent work done by Christians in politics we still have a long way to go. Pornography is still rampant, crime and drugs plague our streets, Marxist revolutions are still being exported by the Soviet Union, and the abortion industry is still booming. Some Christians have shown great heroism in their attempts to counter these evils. Randall Terry, founder and director of Operation Rescue, writes in his book:

> We will have to leave the comfort and safety of our church pews. We are going to have to get our hands dirty, and be active in society. . . . If Christians stay cloistered in their little groups, it's easy to keep unstained by the world. But when we go to the trenches of this life, when we reach out to help the unlovely, we run the risk of being defiled. Involving society, rather than abandoning it, presents a far greater challenge to stay pure. . . . When salt (the Christian influence) stops preserving a nation, that society's going to deteriorate. There's no way around it.[9]

As biblical Christians in the area of politics we must be careful not to be seduced by the evil we are fighting. Jesus Christ warned us not to be overcome by evil, and in the area of politics the end does not justify the means. Christians need to support candidates who will uphold righteousness. They need to become active in both parties and vote for candidates who are in accord with their biblical beliefs.

True Christians of all denominations must create a new vision for the future of America and the world based on the example of Jesus Christ's servanthood. We must not be seduced by evil, partisan politics, unholy alliances, or the mad rush for power. There are millions of young Americans who will be eager to join a coalition based on love and servanthood.

A VISION OF THE CHURCH
OF THE TWENTY-FIRST CENTURY

The church of the twenty-first century will be the authentic New Testament church of the first century made alive and new in the creative power of the Holy Spirit. This church, which has already started to emerge all around the world, will be a healing center for all people and will be characterized by an emphasis on prayer, worship, love of God's Word, and service. It will not be strictly evangelical, fundamentalist, or charismatic, but will be manifest in many different denominations as well as outside denominational structures—any place where believers in Jesus Christ gather to worship God in the power of his Spirit, to study the Word of God, and to move outward in loving service to others.

The following is a list of characteristics that should distinguish God's people in the twenty-first century:

1. A renewed emphasis on praise and worship. The church will be a place of renewed emphasis on praise and worship to the Lord. People will not be afraid to praise God and declare his marvelous deeds. Their worship will be full of gratitude and orderly, not emotionally manipulative. God's people will express intimacy with him in "psalms and hymns and spiritual songs, singing and making melody with your heart to the Lord" (Eph 5:19). Worship should, therefore, be full of life and power.

2. A respect for the Bible as absolute and objective truth. Another characteristic of the emerging church is that it will totally accept the Bible as the final authority in areas that it touches upon. It will encourage all to have a rich under-standing of the Word of God and esteem it.

3. An emphasis on prayer and intercession. The church will recognize and accept its responsibility to pray and intercede for our nation and world. It will gladly accept the role as intercessor and make prayer a priority. The following outline for prayer is taken from a May 5, 1988, National Day of Prayer brochure. The praying church is to:

I. Seek the Lord for the Healing of our Nation

A. Heal and strengthen our homes and families:

Divorce	Youth Rebellion	Child Abuse
Single Parent Families	Lovelessness	Permissiveness
Disunity	Selfishness	Financial Debt

B. Restore the values of society based on biblical morality:

Abortion	Pornography	Judicial System
Racism	Perversion	Law Enforcement
Homosexuality	Anti-Christ Spirit	Education
Secular Humanism	Corruption	Immorality

C. Heal the sick; equip medical science in mercy mission to our nation:

AIDS	Cancer	Medical Research
Doctors	Nurses	Hospitals
Mental Hospitals	Mental Health	Terminally Ill
Medical Schools	Workers	

D. Restore righteous workings in the economics of our nation:

Greed	National Debt	New Jobs
Poverty	Dishonesty	

E. Provide loving and effective care for all people in our nation:

Homeless	Physically Handicapped	Elderly
Immigrants	Mentally Handicapped	Jobless

F. Heal us from the effects of man's attempt to save himself:

Alcoholism	Drug Abuse	Cults
Spiritual Cynicism	New Age	"Self-Helpism"

II. Ask for a Fresh Breath of God's Spirit Bringing

A. A new heart for the people of our nation:

Hope	Peace	Love
Joy	Righteousness	Unity

B. A new vision and moral leadership to our nation:

Direction for Youth	Brotherly Kindness to All
Moral Purity	Mercy to the Needy

C. A new wave of Holy Spirit renewal:

Salvation of the Lost
Purity in the People of God
Fulfillment of the Great Commission
Breaking the Cynicism of Scandal
Breaking Denominational Barriers
Revival in Our Churches
Direction for Evangelism[10]

The church will regularly intercede for these issues and adopt them seriously as goals for the church. By lifting up these needs to the Lord, it will help make them realities.

4. A center of healing. Healing for the physical, emotional, psychological, and spiritual needs of the community will take place in the church. Jesus' commands to pray for the sick will be taken seriously. New Testament healing of body, soul, and spirit will be available through the laying on of hands, prayer from elders, and Christian counseling. All people will be able to receive prayer and comfort. Among these will be those who have diseases such as AIDS.

In addition, all who come to its doors will be welcomed in the love of Jesus Christ. Programs will be provided to help the alcoholic, the drug user, victims of child abuse, the homosexual, the divorced, lonely singles, the elderly, troubled families, teenagers, and others in need. Society's prodigals will make the church their home as will different races, economic groups, and cultures. The love of Jesus Christ will bring unity.

5. A center of ministry to the poor, homeless, and hungry. The church will minister to the poor, homeless, and hungry. Its doors will be open to the handicapped and mentally ill. Poverty, hunger, and homelessness could totally be eliminated from America if every local church would take care of a few of the homeless and destitute. The new church will actively minister to the needs of the community.

6. *A center of creativity.* Welcome will be the artist, intellectual, and creative person. Opportunities will be provided for creative people to minister to the congregation through theater, art, music, poetry, dance, painting, and sculpture. The renewed church will put an emphasis on the creativity of God and his people.

7. *A center of fellowship.* The church will encourage and facilitate life-giving relationships among people to enable them to help each other grow in their life in Christ. Godly relationships built from this kind of interaction will pour out of the church into the community, creating social stability, fidelity in marriage, trustworthiness, and healing.

8. *A center for servanthood.* Characterized by a spirit of servanthood, God's people will work not only to meet the needs of all who come to it, but to minister the life of Jesus Christ by laying down their lives for the needs of others. In practical terms this will mean praying for the community and mobilizing its resources and manpower to assist. The church will not just preach the gospel but it will live the gospel in the midst of a post-Christian culture.

WELCOME TO THE FUTURE

As Christians our destiny is heaven. First Corinthians 2:9 says, "Things which eye has not seen and ear has not heard,

And which have not entered the heart of man, All that God has prepared for those who love Him." The very things modern visionaries and Utopians of the New Age hope to achieve through technology and mysticism, God has waiting for us. For all who have accepted Jesus Christ, Paradise awaits us.

Believers in Jesus Christ are cosmic voyagers who are being prepared to inherit the kingdom of God as priest-kings and joint heirs with Jesus Christ. We will leave our present bodies and put on supernatural bodies which radiate with divine energy. When we have the mind of Christ in its totality, we will be in supernatural communication with one another. Our mental capacities will be substantially enhanced and we will have powers that we currently do not have. Through the powerful redemptive work of Jesus Christ, all believers will reach their full human potential. The secular humanistic efforts at reaching human potential here on earth will look ridiculously feeble in comparison. Each person will be released to be everything he or she was created to be. There will be a creative explosion inside every individual that will cause people to be free for the first time in their lives.

Our new home in heaven will have no air pollution or waste. The light in heaven will be more glorious than any sunrise or sunset you have ever seen. "And the city has no need of the sun or of the moon to shine upon it, for the glory of God has illumined it, and its lamp is the Lamb" (Rv 21:23). This light will not only illuminate in the visual sense but it will be the light of pure love and it will perpetually thrill the soul. There will be a supernatural invigorating force of joy, peace, and glory radiating from Christ. Our experiences in

God's presence here on earth are only a foretaste of the future kingdom. The human nature locked into this present earthly body is not built to contain the fullness of God's Spirit in the way our new bodies in heaven will be able to.

God wants to illuminate the consciousness of his people and give them a vision for what is to be theirs in heaven. For in the eternal or timeless scheme of things we are moving quickly to this appointed hour. Romans 8:18-22 says:

> For I consider that the sufferings of this present time are not worthy to be compared with the glory that is to be revealed to us. For the anxious longing of creation waits eagerly for the revealing of the sons of God. For the creation was subjected to futility, not of its own will, but because of Him who subjected it, in hope that the creation itself also will be set free from its slavery to corruption into the freedom of the glory of the children of God. For we know that the whole creation groans and suffers the pains of childbirth together until now.

All of creation is in labor. The very universe—the stars, the galaxies, the mountains, forests, rivers, streams, and flowers— is straining to burst into its eternal cosmic beauty. But it is waiting for us who are in Christ to be revealed as the sons and daughters of God.

Hebrews 2:3-5 states:

> How shall we escape if we neglect so great a salvation? After it was at the first spoken through the Lord, it was confirmed to us by those who heard, God also bearing witness with them, both by signs and wonders and by

various miracles and by gifts of the Holy Spirit according to His own will. For He did not subject to angels the world to come. . . .

Our salvation is great because we are going to be in a new universe that glows with the splendor of the living God. God is confirming future reality by signs and wonders in our present day, as well as by the gifts of the Holy Spirit. Don't shy away from such things; God is proving his goodness toward us and demonstrating his love. Don't neglect his great salvation. Receive it in its fullness, and bear witness to it in every aspect of your life. Alive in the Holy Spirit, ready and willing to meet people's needs and to fight for their lives, standing for the kingdom of God, we as transformed Christians can begin to meet the challenge of reclaiming our world for Christ.

Paul McGuire
P.O. Box 713
Hollywood, California 90078

New Age and Biblical Worldviews

O UR CONCEPTION OF GOD determines our worldview. We are shaped by what we worship. As Virgil said, "We make our destinies by our choice of gods." Thus, New Age and Christian ideas about God are reflected in their view of humanity. When God is conceived as a nonpersonal energy force, humanity is similarly conceived. When we believe God to be what he says he is, we will see ourselves as we are. Without a clear picture of God, we will see nothing clearly.

The following chart by Brooks Alexander and Robert Burrows of the Spiritual Counterfeits Project is intended to illustrate the difference between New Age and biblical worldviews and also to illustrate the internal logic and coherency of the worldviews themselves.

The chart adapted from SCP Newsletter 10:5, © 1985. Robert Burrows is editor-in-chief of the *SCP Newsletter,* and Brooks Alexander is director of the Spiritual Counterfeits Project, Berkeley, California. Printed by permission of Spiritual Counterfeits Project, P.O. Box 4308, Berkeley, California 94704. This chart begins on page 160 and continues to page 165.

New Age vs. Biblical Worldviews Chart

NEW AGE WORLDVIEW	BIBLICAL WORLDVIEW
GOD'S NATURE	
1. Ultimate reality (god) is One and impersonal. Being One, it contains no distinctions, is undifferentiated, without qualities or attributes. It cannot be personal, since personality is a by-product of differentiation and distinction.	**1.** God is personal and has attributes appropriate to personality: will, purpose, values, concerns, freedom, creativity, and responsiveness. These attributes are reflected in all that God is and does.
CREATION	
2. God *emanates* (not creates) the cosmos out of its own being. There is no distinction or discontinuity between god and the cosmos: all is one. God is creation.	**2.** God *creates* the cosmos out of nothing. God transcends his creation and is distinct from it. The cosmos is not God and does not share his essential being.
3. The emanations of god—the cosmos—are appearances which have only a limited and deceptive reality. The full reality behind all appearances is the One, which does not allow particularity of existence in any form, by definition.	**3.** The creation is both real and good. When God created *ex nihilo*—out of nothing—he brought a genuine novelty into existence. The creation is now flawed and fallen. Even so, it continues to display the imprint of its Creator and remains in God's sight "very good." In the end, God will renew it, not reject it.

NEW AGE WORLDVIEW	BIBLICAL WORLDVIEW
HUMANITY	
4. Humanity also is not distinct from god. Human beings, like the rest of the cosmos, are in essence made out of god. Like ultimate reality, they are reduced to pure consciousness, featureless and impersonal.	**4.** Humanity is part of creation. We share its reality and goodness. Human beings are created to grow and develop in personhood, because God himself is personal.
5. Human beings, therefore, have no innate attributes or inherent limitations. Human nature is not fixed in any regard, but is changeable and infinitely flexible. Humanity therefore has infinite potential. Human beings inherently embody all the power, knowledge, and wisdom of the cosmos, as well as its divine nature. Humanity is god.	**5.** Human beings, therefore, have a particular design that provides for individual development. The limitations of finite existence are boundaries which provide for true freedom. The limitations of created existence are intended, designed, and blessed by God. This also means that human beings are distinct from and subject to God. No created thing can bear the burden of divinity. Humanity is not God.
DEATH	
6. Divine humanity has no limits. Mortality is unreal. Death is the final state of growth; it resembles termination only from the viewpoint of the illusory, separate self. Death is a process within the illusory cosmos and is therefore an	**6.** In addition to the providential boundaries of created existence, further limits were introduced by sin. Many of the limits we experience are the result of the curse that followed the Fall (Genesis 3:14-19). Death in particular raises a

NEW AGE WORLDVIEW	BIBLICAL WORLDVIEW
DEATH	
6. (cont.) illusion as well. The impersonal ground of existence is deathless and unchanging. Human beings are therefore immortal. Ultimately, death does not exist.	**6.** (cont.) baffling barrier to the human quest for meaning. Death's reign is universal, and it nullifies hope and achievement. Death is God's judgment on sin and is therefore real and inescapable.
KNOWING GOD	
7. Humanity's link with ultimate reality is based on the oneness of all existence and its essential unity with the divine.	**7.** Humanity's connection with God is through communion in relationship. The distinction between God and his creation permits an appropriate and fulfilling relationship. God created us to know him, endowing us with personhood—his image— to this end.
8. The human dilemma is a constriction of awareness that we are god. We have limited our consciousness so we do not perceive the One, but only fragments of it.	**8.** The dilemma of humanity is a broken relationship with God. Our ancestors were dismissed from God's presence. All their descendants, including us, are likewise born into spiritual exile. Our sin makes us enemies of God. We have lost the very relationship in which we were designed to find fulfillment.
9. The limitations on our awareness are imposed by	**9.** The source of our loss of relationship with God is sin

NEW AGE WORLDVIEW	BIBLICAL WORLDVIEW
KNOWING GOD	
9. (cont.) social conditioning. We are taught to break reality up into good and bad, us and them, me and you, and so on. As we move into adulthood, these mental systems become more sophisticated, but no less divisive. Self, family, nation, race, and "matter" all define illusory boundaries where in fact there is only Oneness. Reason and belief-systems that limit reality must be swept away.	**9.** (cont.) and rebellion. Rebellion, freely willed, has poisoned our gene pool. We continually turn our backs on God, not just with indifference, but with hostility. The life of Jesus clearly demonstrates that if God plants himself lovingly in our midst, we will resort to murder to remove him. That is who we are. We are caught in a situation of our own making, and we are powerless to unmake it.
SIN	
10. The effects of seeing reality in pieces are numerous and negative. Subjectively, we experience the anxiety and alienation of illusory separateness. Division, hostility, and conflict emerge as alienation is projected onto other, equally illusory "selves," thus deepening and multiplying the mistake. All the hate and miseries we see around us come from the error of attributing reality to separate, limited, individual existence.	**10.** Sin is rebellion that results in death. Sin fragments, separates, and alienates human beings. It divides us from God and deepens our spiritual blindness. We begin by rejecting God's presence; we end by denying his reality. Sin also divides people, internally, against themselves and against one another. It is useless to talk of people solving their own problems so long as they are infected with sin; for it is sin's nature to divide people and turn them against one another.

NEW AGE WORLDVIEW	BIBLICAL WORLDVIEW
SALVATION	
11. The remedy for our dilemma is to attain knowledge of divine reality—the One. Such knowledge is widely known and goes by many names—gnosis, enlightenment, god-consciousness. Whatever it is called, it represents a return to the source, union of dualities, fusion with the One, and transcendence of human nature to self-divinity.	**11.** The healing of our sinful condition depends on the restoration of our broken relationship with God. There are no techniques to apply, no procedures to learn. As the dilemma is personal and relational, so is its resolution. Healing is initiated by God, and is accepted by human choice. On the human side, acceptance of God's forgiveness involves "repentance," the simple acknowledgement of what was previously ignored: our creatureliness and dependence on God, and especially our rebellion and hostility against God.
12. The self is both the subject and the agent of enlightenment. Self-realization, as enlightenment is sometimes known, is precisely that—knowledge of the self by the self. Yet the self, as *ego* or *persona*, is also the source of the problem. It must be undone so the Superself—the One—may emerge and be known. Awareness of the One is accessible only to those who can step outside ordinary modes of perception into altered	**12.** Repentance is not the source of salvation. Salvation is a gift. Repentance is the act of accepting that gift. The gift is God's reconciling love demonstrated in Christ, who bore our hostility and rose to undo our due judgment: death itself. The gospel is the news of that gift. The entire process of restoration is personal and relational, from its conception in the mind of God to its acceptance or rejection in the minds

NEW AGE WORLDVIEW	BIBLICAL WORLDVIEW
SALVATION	
12. (cont.) states of consciousness which dispel the illusory boundaries of individual existence. Therefore, the self applies to itself techniques of manipulation that finally dissolve its own existence.	**12.** (cont.) and hearts of people.
ULTIMATE GOAL	
13. Union with the One results in the dissolution of existence in general and of identity and personhood in particular. In effect, enlightenment repeals the curse of life by embracing the curse of death. It ends the alienation of personal existence by ending the existence of the person.	**13.** Salvation repeals the curse of death by restoring our relationship with God. When our relationship with God is restored, our personhood is affirmed, healed, and fulfilled. Our guilt and alienation from God are erased, while our individuality is not lost or weakened. The purpose of the gospel is that we are cleansed, not disposed; restored, not rejected; strengthened, not extinguished.

Chapter Notes

Chapter One
The Search

1. Marilyn Ferguson, *The Aquarian Conspiracy*, (Los Angeles: J.P. Tarcher, Inc., 1980), p. 49.
2. Ferguson, *The Aquarian Conspiracy*, quoted from bookjacket.
3. Ferguson, *The Aquarian Conspiracy*, p. 417.
4. Les Donaldson, *Behavioral Supervision*, (Redding, Massachusetts: Addison-Wesley Publishing Co., 1980), from the Preface.
5. Laura Torbet, "The Whole Mind Newsletter," *Omni*, October 1987, p. 131.
6. Marc MacNamara, "The Return of Werner Erhard Guru II," *Los Angeles Magazine*, May 1988, p. 109
7. MacNamara, "The Return of Werner Erhard Guru II," p. 109.
8. MacNamara, "The Return of Werner Erhard Guru II," p. 111.
9. MacNamara, "The Return of Werner Erhard Guru II," p. 112.
10. Ruth C. Clark, "Pentagon Meditation Club," *Meditation*, Fall 1988, p. 7.
11. Clark, "Pentagon Meditation Club," p. 7.
12. Karl Schoenberger, "In Okinawa, Supernatural Is Taken Very Seriously," *Los Angeles Times*, September 3, 1988, p. 8.
13. Art Kunkin, "Kuhuna: 'There Are No Limits!'" *Whole Life Times*, June 1988, p. 7.
14. Paul Andrews and Art Kunkin, An Interview with Lynn Andrews: "Opening the Shamanic Teaching," *Whole Life Times*, August 1988, p. 10.
15. Andrews and Kunkin, "Opening the Shamanic Teaching," p. 10.
16. Art Kunkin, An Interview with Diane Parrinello: "The Strange Story of Starlink," *Whole Life Times*, June 1988, p. 13.
17. Kunkin, "The Strange Story of Starlink," p. 13.
18. Ad in *Conscious Living*, May 1988, p. 2.

Chapter Two
Overview of the New Age

1. J. Quigley and L. Zuckerman, "The First Lady's Astrologer," *Time,* May 16, 1988, p. 41.
2. Art Kunkin, "The Most Famous Astrologer of the Twentieth Century," *Whole Life Times,* May 1988, p. 14.
3. Otto Friedrich, "New Age Harmonies," *Time,* December 7, 1987, p. 65.
4. Tom Peters and Nancy Austin, *A Passion for Excellence,* (New York: Random House, 1985), pp. 7, 10-11.
5. David Spangler, "Defining the New Age," *New Realities,* June 1988, p. 29.
6. Allan Baughn, "Kevin Ryerson: The Thinking Man's Channel," *New Realities,* June 1988, p. 32.

Chapter Three
Spiritual Gifts and Supernatural Power

1. Anthony Robbins, *Unlimited Power: The Way to Peak Personal Achievement,* (New York: Ballantine Books, 1986), bookjacket.

Chapter Four
Multi-Dimensional Warfare

1. Francis Schaeffer, *The Great Evangelical Disaster,* (Westchester, Illinois: Crossway Books, 1984), pp. 23-24.
2. Nikos Kazantzakis, *Report to Greco,* (New York: Simon and Schuster, 1961), p. 320.
3. Interview with M. Scott Peck, *Omni,* October 1988, p. 126.

Chapter Five
Taking Authority over the New Age

1. Francis Schaeffer, *The Great Evangelical Disaster,* pp. 23-24.

Chapter Six
Reclaiming Our World for Christ

1. George Gallup, Jr. and William Proctor, *Forecast 2000*, New York: William Morrow and Co., 1984), p. 151.
2. "More Christians Are Saying No to Church," *Christianity Today*, September 2, 1958, p. 56.
3. "More Christians Are Saying No to Church," *Christianity Today*, September 2, 1958, p. 56.
4. J. Stillson Judah, *Hare Krishna and the Counterculture*, (New York: John Wiley and Son, Inc., 1974), pp. 147-151.
5. Demos Shakarian, *Vision*, 1987, p. 3.
6. Quote from the "Pastors' Conference" at The Church on the Way, Van Nuys, California, 1987.
7. Cal Thomas, "Cursing Darkness Sells Devil's Product," *Los Angeles Times*, Friday, August 12, 1988.
8. Judith Michaelson, "Fight over Public TV Pie: Independent Producers Want a Bigger Slice," *Los Angeles Times*, June 24, 1988, pt. 6, p. 1.
9. Randall Terry, *Operation Rescue*, (Springdale, Pennsylvania: Whitaker House, 1988), p. 52.
10. *National Day of Prayer Brochure*, Church on the Way, Van Nuys, California, May 5, 1988.

Other Books of Interest
from Servant Publications

The Third Wave of the Holy Spirit
Encountering the Power of Signs and Wonders Today
C. Peter Wagner

What is the Third Wave of the Holy Spirit? In the early 1900s, the Holy Spirit rocked the church in what is known as the pentecostal movement. In the middle of this century, the charismatic renewal brought great revival to mainline churches. Now in the 1980s, the sick are being healed, the lame are walking, and demons are being cast out. Peter Wagner calls this the Third Wave of the Holy Spirit and introduces the reader to this dynamic new movement of God. An exciting and fascinating introduction to the Third Wave by a prominent expert on church growth at Fuller Theological Seminary. *$6.95*

Signs, Wonders, and the Kingdom of God
A Biblical Guide for the Reluctant Skeptic
Don Williams

This new book on signs and wonders presents a fascinating, biblical theology of the kingdom of God. Dr. Williams describes how God works to establish his reign now and in eternity and how we can demonstrate and proclaim, as Jesus did, the supernatural power of his kingdom.

Signs, Wonders, and the Kingdom of God investigates the relationship between supernatural power and the ministry of the church today. As a community of love and faith under the reign of God, we can continue Jesus' ministry of power, evangelizing the poor, casting out demons, healing the sick, and setting free the captives. A compelling look at the kingdom of God from the perspective of signs and wonders. *$7.95*